Praise for *It Happened!*

"Jim Lampley's book is an unforgettable ride down memory lane for serious and even casual sports fans. He not only saw the great games, he called them. He not only met the great athletes, he befriended them. For over 40 years he was there—on the sidelines, at ringside, in the locker rooms, in the press boxes, and he didn't miss many of the after game parties. A rollicking feast for sports fans."

—John Grisham, bestselling author and novelist

"An epic career has placed Jim Lampley at the scene of some of sport's most memorable moments—moments enhanced by the way he described them. That career also led to relationships with many of the most significant and fascinating figures in modern sports history, and those interactions inform the anecdotes and insights in Jim's engaging memoir."

—Bob Costas, Broadcasting Legend

"I called dozens of big fights with Jim Lampley, and from that I learned to expect that he would call my fights with passion and emotional truth. On November 5, 1994, I knocked out Michael Moorer and gave Jim the platform to create the title of this book. Enjoy the story."

—George Foreman, Three-Time World Heavyweight Boxing Champion and HBO Boxing Ringside Analyst

"*It Happened* is the Jim Lampley story and what a story it is! Jim is one of the greatest sports broadcasters of all time and his call of legendary boxing matches will forever be part of sports history. We first met at an ABC Sports *Superstars* taping in 1975. Thirteen years later he became the host of HBO's weekday Wimbledon telecasts, and a major part of HBO's groundbreaking tennis shows. Jim is a great colleague, a great friend, and a joy to work with, and this book is a great read."

—Billie Jean King, Iconic Founder of Women's Sport Foundation

"As a member of the production staff for NBC's Olympics coverage, I was honored to write in Jim Lampley's voice at the Olympics in Sydney, Salt Lake City, and Athens. There are few sports television voices as passionate, informed, and memorable as Lampley's. He spent a half century telling compelling stories about others, and now he is finally telling his own remarkable story."

—Daniel Goldman, United States Congressman, New York State

"I joined Jim Lampley calling swim races on ABC for years and shared a highly rated Olympics late-night studio show with him in 1984. No male sportscaster was ever more helpful and fairer to women athletes as well as women in the sports business than Jim. He always added a significant dimension to every sport he covered."

—Donna de Varona, Olympic Gold Medalist Swimmer and Women's Sports Pioneer

"No one—and I mean no one—is better equipped to write about televised sports over the past years from the inside on a personal level than Jim Lampley."

—Thomas Hauser, Author, *Muhammad Ali: A Tribute To The Greatest*

"When I was moving toward the heavyweight championship as the first legitimate British contender in several decades, Jim Lampley was objective and HBO gave me a fair shake. I never worried he wouldn't give me credit for what I could do, and that helped me fulfill my potential. This is the colorful story of Jim's long romance with my sport."

—Lennox Lewis, Three-Time Heavyweight Boxing Champion

"From boy wonder to veteran sage, with total recall of everything, Jim Lampley knocks us out with the story of his journey. You done good, old friend!"

—Larry Merchant, HBO Commentator and Celebrated Sports Journalist

"When ABC Sports hired me to write seven volumes of Olympic research manuals, my boss shared this piece of wisdom: 'Only three people will read every word you write: your mother, me, and Jim Lampley.' That was true, except I am not sure my mother made it past volume one."

—Draggan Mihailovich, Producer, CBS *60 Minutes*

IT HAPPENED!

IT HAPPENED!

A Uniquely Lucky Life in Sports Television

JIM LAMPLEY

with ART CHANSKY

Matt Holt Books
An Imprint of BenBella Books, Inc.
Dallas, TX

It Happened! copyright © 2025 by Jim Lampley and Art Chansky

Matt Holt is an imprint of BenBella Books, Inc.
8080 N. Central Expressway
Suite 1700
Dallas, TX 75206
benbellabooks.com
Send feedback to feedback@benbellabooks.com

BenBella and *Matt Holt* are federally registered trademarks.

Printed in the United States of America
10 9 8 7 6 5 4 3 2 1

Library of Congress Control Number: 2024047599
ISBN 9781637746431 (hardcover)
ISBN 9781637746448 (electronic)

Copyediting by Scott Calamar
Proofreading by Sarah Vostok and Denise Pangia
Text design and composition by Jordan Koluch
Cover design by Brigid Pearson
Cover photo by Ed Mulholland, courtesy of HBO
Printed by Lake Book Manufacturing

This is in honor of my mother, Peggy Lampley,
and my grandmother Mildred Askew Lampley,
who spent three decades competing for my attention by telling me stories,
which stimulated everything that has happened to me since.

Contents

Foreword: The Sweet Science

No televised sport is more dependent on its dissection and interpretation by a descriptive analyst for the audience than boxing. It is a lonely sport, dominated largely by the socially desperate, seeking solace from the dangers and temptations of the street inside a boxing gym.

To the casual observer, it is two men (or women) pounding each other in the face and body until one succumbs or a bell rings to mark completion. But to devout fans of "the sweet science," it is an intricate chess match of feints and slips, a war of footwork and positioning. At its highest level it is a violent ballet—technique and craft and the transfer of energy from a back foot through a fist, ultimately landing like thunder on an opponent's chin.

But aside from the occasional fight showcasing the occasional fighter who transcended the sport—the Muhammad Alis, the Sugar Ray Leonards—boxing receded through the golden decades of American sports television into the shadows: too violent, its combatants' paths too checkered, until...

HBO's World Championship Boxing would reintroduce mainstream America to the sweet science through a combination of brilliant promotion of the fighters' personalities and—more importantly—a decision to educate the audience rather than to dumb boxing down. Viewers were invited to become experts, to learn how to appreciate the sport's unique culture, eventually to understand the brilliance of a Julio Cesar Chavez, the scientific violence of a Mike Tyson, the unique intelligence of a Floyd Mayweather. And eventually, our professor would be Jim Lampley.

Through a career built on educating the audience in the "What the hell is this?" esoterica of *ABC's Wide World of Sports*, where his range was tested amid everything from the grandeur of downhill skiing to the folksiness of the World Lumberjack Championships, to his vast range of experiences at 14 Olympics, Lampley became an expert in teaching the details of sports *as those sports were unfolding*. No easy task to get an audience invested in a thing they might not have known was a thing until they started watching the thing...

Applied to boxing at a time when some of the most electrifying fighters were emerging, Jim took us along on his own learning journey, deftly picking the brains of the "experts" working with him, be it Roy Jones Jr., Bernard Hopkins, or Emanuel Steward. Jim developed a unique ability to recognize a feat the layman may not fully appreciate, then explain why that feat was impressive without ever being condescending to the audience.

It is a rare gift, one that required a genuine passion for the sport, as well as a real appreciation for both the competitor and the spectator—Jim was almost desperate that we should understand the feat, knowing our growing knowledge of the sport would magnify our experience of the fights.

Looking back, Jim Lampley guided us through many of the most electrifying and memorable fights of the last 40 years, from the unbeatable Mike Tyson's fall at the fists of Buster Douglas through George Foreman's age-defying return to the heavyweight pinnacle with his knockout of unbeaten Michael Moorer, a moment marked by the exclamation "It happened!"—now the poetic title of this book.

From pioneering on the sidelines to hosting Super Bowls, three decades of Olympics and 31 years at ringside, Jim Lampley's voice wrote captions for countless triumphs and tragedies, always building on the education he was given amid ABC's "thrill of victory and agony of defeat" culture.

I have enjoyed lengthy conversations with Jim about fights he called—pick one, let's say De La Hoya versus Trinidad, and it is as though he recalls every meaningful punch, every duck or slip, the determination in the fighters' eyes, the pleading cheers from the family in the third row—he remembers all of it.

So with his passion he feeds our passion. This book is a conversation with Jim Lampley as he relives the moments we all witnessed and the circumstances that placed him there. We add more understanding and our appreciation grows. I have spoken with Jim for hours, together reliving fights from years, even decades ago, then looked back at the event (thank you, YouTube) and there's his voice. And I'm as excited again to witness the event as the thousands in the arena. Eager to hear him guide me through the spectacle. And I sit back, and the spectacle is even greater than I remembered.

—Taylor Sheridan

Prologue

Jim Lampley and the reason "It Happened" (Courtesy of Will Hart)

gathered my first impressions of George Foreman at the same moment when millions of other Americans did, in the closing days of the 1968 Mexico City Olympics as he drew attention for waving a tiny American flag in the ring after winning the heavyweight boxing gold medal.

It was only 10 days after American sprinters Tommie Smith and John

Carlos had elicited a distinctly different public response by posing on the medal stand in a side-by-side Black Power salute after their respective gold- and bronze-winning performances in the 200-meter run. Heads bowed, gloved fists extended skyward during the national anthem, Smith and Carlos made clear they thought it was important to send one message about American society, for which they were banished from the Olympics. Foreman had sent another, obviously more mainstream.

Smith and Carlos were college students at San José State, and that graphically affected how they saw their responsibility within American culture. Foreman had left the crime and poverty of Houston's Fifth Ward and migrated to Pleasanton, California, not far from San Jose, to enter the Job Corps, where he took up amateur boxing. He went on to overpower a veteran Russian heavyweight to win Olympic gold and returned to America a newly stamped hero. His feelings differed markedly—if not understandably—from those of Smith and Carlos.

Foreman was 19. So was I, watching in my mother's apartment living room in Miami, where I had returned after three humiliating semesters and part of a fourth at the University of North Carolina in Chapel Hill. My uncontrollable appetites for beer and sleep had left me on the brink of flunking out before hitchhiking home to try to get my hopeless act together after losing my car, Mom's 1964 Oldsmobile Cutlass, and my entire collection of rhythm-and-blues music at all-night poker games at the SAE fraternity house.

Neither of us could have foreseen the paths along which we would converge over the next 26 years. A fiction writer couldn't have dreamed it up. But through an interlocking series of surprise circumstances, it happened, and spontaneously came to be commemorated in those surprises. It's a story so filled with bizarre coincidences and irrational reversals that if I hadn't lived it, I might not believe it is true. But trust me...it happened.

Prologue

And at this point it wouldn't make sense not to record it on paper. So here it is.

It's the story of how my life constantly and repeatedly rescued itself from self-destruction and left me with identities and encounters that are in some ways unique for an American sportscaster. It's a five-decade kaleidoscope of inexplicable good fortune, terrible misjudgment, and disasters averted on the fly. It's a hard-to-believe catalog mirroring the 70-year evolution of network television sports coverage in America. It's not just my story, but by association the story of many of the planet's greatest athletes and broadcasters, past and present. And there are moments when any rational reader is likely to think, *Wow. Is this true?*

It's all true. There were witnesses all along the way. I wouldn't risk the embarrassment of putting it into words if that weren't the case. I'm grateful, and in some ways humbled, and still astonished, that it happened. It truly did.

Introduction

First Lucky Break

The vast majority of team sports telecasts on all forms of television these days feature one or two reporters on the sidelines. But it wasn't always that way.

Through the early 1970s, baseball, football, and basketball broadcasts signed on with two, usually ancient, talking heads, filling the frames that greeted audiences. Until ABC executive producer Roone Arledge had another idea.

Trying to attract a younger audience to his weekly nationally televised college football games, Arledge wanted to add a new dimension to veterans Keith Jackson and iconic former Oklahoma football coach Bud Wilkinson, who was well into his late 50s, then considered an advanced age.

Arledge invented the idea of having a college-age reporter on the football sideline. He conducted a search of college campuses around the country, and ABC wound up with 432 candidates. That number remains indelible in my mind, since I was among them and one of the two who got the job at the age of 25.

Arledge, who died in 2002, might have had the idea before 1974, when

I walked down the boat dock along the Tennessee River next to Neyland Stadium in Knoxville to introduce the college football season opener between Tennessee and UCLA. But there was a technology issue, which Arledge and ABC inadvertently, and under tragic circumstances, had discovered how to solve at the 1972 Olympics in Munich.

Howard Cosell and Peter Jennings were in West Germany covering the Summer Olympic Games when nine Israeli athletes were kidnapped and two murdered by the Black September Palestinian militant organization. The broadcasters were pressed into the most challenging assignment of their careers.

They wanted to get closer to where the athletes were being held hostage to film what they saw and broadcast it live to a national audience. Cosell and Jennings were harping about the inability of any kind of broadcast signal to penetrate structures like the concrete walls in Munich, but their crew tried anyway, and learned what the wireless microphones could do. They were able to get the story back to the production truck and on to America from there.

With this discovery, ABC convened a meeting in New York of Sports, News, and Entertainment chieftains to discuss what could be done. And the first idea was "we can put a reporter on the sideline of a football game." That became the entry point for my 50-year career as a network television sportscaster.

1

The Four As

Television's first sideline sports reporter

Thursday, August 8, 1974, was already a momentous day in American history by the time Linda Lee Lampley and I arrived via automobile ride in Swan Corner, North Carolina, to set up in a rental house for the weekend. We were the guests of our good friends Buck and Kay Goldstein, whose job had been to locate and rent an inviting beach house for a three-day late-summer weekend out of Chapel Hill, where Linda and I were UNC grad students.

It was never a bad idea to put ourselves in the care of the Goldsteins. They were organizers.

By late afternoon to early evening, Kay had deciphered directions from a real estate agent, and we arrived. The next objective would be to locate the right seafood restaurant. And that, too, would be up to Buck and Kay.

Linda and I were focused on the radio reports we had heard on the afternoon trip. More than two years after the shocking break-in at the Democratic National Committee headquarters in Washington, DC's Watergate complex, and as the result of the historic investigation that had substantiated his role to cover it up, President Richard Nixon announced his intention to resign and fly off to private life in San Clemente, California. And the following day, August 9, Gerald R. Ford would become president.

So our arrival in Swan Corner Thursday, or the following day, would rank along with November 22, 1963, the date of John F. Kennedy's assassination, as the most momentous day of history in my 25-year lifetime. Even if we had seen it coming, and in Linda's and my case we certainly hoped we had, it was stunning.

We were almost out the door when the phone on the wall in the kitchen rang. Since the Goldsteins were the lessors of record for the weekend, Buck stepped around the kitchen counter and answered the phone.

"Hello." A brief wait. "Yes, he's here right now. Who shall I say is calling?"

I was the only "he" who could be the subject. Whatever this was, it didn't at first seem to be good. Just two days before, I had received certification from the University of North Carolina Department of Radio, Television, and Motion Pictures (RTVMP) that I completed all the necessary courses—11 of them—to earn a master's degree. That left me one step—a thesis—short of the degree that would culminate in one of the most unlikely comebacks imaginable for a student who as a sophomore had held a 1.44 academic average that placed me on the verge of being expelled from my dream alma mater.

Right at an academic death's door, I had reversed direction and made my first two undergraduate A grades in laborious correspondence courses to retrieve the right to show up again on campus and continue my redemption. I had escaped from a dreary bank file room in sweaty Miami to return to the paradise of Chapel Hill and begin earning the long string of As that convinced an influential professor and department head to give me a scholarship to pursue a master's degree in RTVMP.

Then came the moment when RTVMP chairman Dr. Wesley Wallace told me ABC Sports was beginning a process to hire a college-age reporter on the sidelines of their iconic college football telecasts. The network was planning to conduct interviews across the country, and the university wanted to present me as a candidate. He was solicitous enough to ask if I might be interested in that.

The concept was innovative enough that, from the beginning, ABC Sports seemed aware that it might get a lot of young people's hopes up and break hearts, even as it began down the road toward doing exactly that. They billboarded from the beginning that it would be a nationwide search, and hundreds of candidates would be screened. The candidates would be college age, theoretically 18 to 22, with little or no background as television professionals. Interviews would be held at 16 locations so that no geographic region would be left out.

The initial screening would lead to a second step, in which a number of aspirants (maybe a handful, maybe a dozen, maybe more) would do some form of taped audition. The ultimate survivor of the search would show up on the college football telecasts for that season, 1974, and then there would be a repeat search for a new college-age reporter the following year, and on forward year to year from there.

As it turned out, predictably, some of that was true and some of it went the way of all flesh. To begin with, as I pointed out to Dr. Wallace, I was 24, about to turn 25, and I had done a lot of on-air work. Crafty as he was from his deep background in broadcasting, Dr. Wallace said, "Frankly, you don't look that old, and those are exactly the reasons they would be crazy not to choose you. They just haven't thought it all through yet." Later I learned he had convinced the journalism and athletic departments not to recommend any other candidates, so the university would not be diluting my chances.

My first screening was in mid-May at the Parliament House Hotel in downtown Birmingham. I had no place to stay in Birmingham, and the appointment was for 9 AM, so I chose to drive overnight. I got to the Parliament House with about a half hour to spare. It was going to be a hot, sweltering Alabama day. I was wearing my best discount suit and a pair of shoes with stacked heels that made me appear an inch and a half taller.

Thirty-six of us were seated in rows of chairs in a large conference room. Conscious of my slightly advanced age amid all the fresh-faced undergraduates, I took a seat in the back row and tried to hide. We waited. And waited.

After a 30-minute lull, three people burst into the room. I was instantly impressed with their level of self-assurance. Or intimidated by their level of self-assurance. Perhaps both. Though unaware at the time, I was getting my first taste of the cocky self-congratulation that went with working for one of the three major commercial television networks, more specifically working for ABC Sports. ABC was not the equal of CBS or NBC in news or entertainment, but under the leadership of Roone Arledge, the visionary executive, it was overwhelmingly dominant in sports. It appeared the three young people who had walked in were not just aware of that but driven by it.

Though blond associate producer Terry Jastrow and brunette production assistant Barbara Roche were impressive, Dick Ebersol did most of the speaking. We soon learned he was Arledge's administrative assistant, and that they all had a rollicking night reacquainting themselves with the watering holes they knew from covering Alabama versus Auburn football games. According to Dick, it was just another rip-roaring evening on what was so far turning out to be one hell of a tour, and they were now about halfway through. The implication was clear: *Wouldn't you give your left arm to be one of us?* Of course.

I had seen privileged preppies at UNC, the kind you meet at the Delta Kappa Epsilon house or at lacrosse player parties. So Ebersol's background was written all over him. His lengthy dishwater hair was dripping wet and had been pushed, not brushed, off his forehead. A pair of Ray-Ban Wayfarers placed on top held it in place. His white oxford-cloth Brooks Brothers button-down was half tucked in, half front shirttail out of his faded Levi's, one knee thoroughly ripped out. The sole of one expensive oxblood penny loafer was secured to the moccasin by a healthy wrapping of adhesive tape. That was a "Yale grad" identifier. I had dealt in this ethos during summers in the rich Hendersonville suburb of Flat Rock, North Carolina, sometimes with success.

The spiel bore repetitive references to the notion this whole thing was special because "it is really Roone's idea." That sounded promising, for reasons I wasn't about to share with anyone quite yet. What wasn't promising came next, when the 36 of us drew numbers from a fishbowl to determine the order of five- to seven-minute interviews that would for the moment decide our fates. I drew number 34. A quick calculation told me I had a three- to four-hour wait to come.

It was boiling outside. There was a limited amount of seating in the lobby. I was 25 years old among 35 undergraduates. Ebersol had told us all about meeting a guy at Stanford who was the Associated Press (AP) stringer on the grounds of the Hearst mansion, living in a tent from day one through to the end of Patty Hearst's captivity, filing the national news lead story many times in that span. The premier candidate for the position had made it quite difficult for Ebersol to imagine they would see someone better. His name was Don Tollefson, the editor of the *Stanford Daily* and on-site AP reporter on the day the Hearst kidnapping story had broken. That was only one of several credentials Ebersol acknowledged to all of us in Birmingham he was enthralled with, and it was more than enough to make clear to me the once-in-a-lifetime college football dream job was out of reach.

I was regretting the seven-hour drive down and dreading the ride back even more. And any extended departure from North Carolina, like getting the gig, would cause me to miss a lot of Tar Heels football and basketball games.

So I entered the smaller room to face the three of them in a defeatist mode. Jastrow had an ingratiating grin and an even more ingratiating Junior Chamber of Commerce style. He began. "So, tell us what you think of our little project here?"

"I think it is the most ridiculous load of crap I have ever heard."

Shock. And who knows, maybe awe, too.

"Pardon me?"

"Well, the idea that you are going around the country to interview more than 400 supposed candidates for this, and from that evidence you are going to choose 'the face and voice of the American college student,' is insulting to all of us. Even to whoever gets picked. I can't believe I wasted my time."

Later someone showed me the one-page evaluation form on which Ebersol had written about me: "Alienated, Arrogant, Abrasive,

Antagonistic." It became known in the ABC college football production truck as "the four As."

So at the end of the first round in May 1974, they had more than 400 resumes and face-to-face evaluations of very young people who might conceivably be candidates for other positions at ABC Sports. I began getting invited to board airplanes and go to New York to interview for jobs—real jobs, not college-age reporters—they were trying to fill.

One was in program planning, to specifically research telecast rights to all the obscure and unusual sports events, literally around the world, that fed the weekly machine of *ABC's Wide World of Sports*. I flew to New York in mid-July for an interview, which was thrillingly perfunctory. They had already made up their minds and offered me the job.

And now, one week into August, I was in a rented beach house, secured under a name other than mine, in a remote corner of North Carolina I had never even heard of, and Buck Goldstein was on the phone with someone looking to talk to me.

"Sure, I'll get him. Jim, it's Dick Ebersol." Amid my shock, I had nothing but the worst expectations.

Ebersol was strikingly polite. He was apologetic about interrupting what he guessed was a relaxing getaway as I prepared to move to New York. He wanted me to know he had been thinking of me ever since our face to face in Alabama and had followed with interest my progress through the division's series of steps toward hiring me. He could only imagine how delighted I was with that opportunity, given what he knew about my grad school transcript. But now something unexpected had arisen.

"The world doesn't yet know, and I doubt anyone has told you, that we made our decision on the college-age reporter position, and we have told

Don Tollefson to get ready to be in Knoxville September 7 for UCLA vs. Tennessee. But as we considered that, Roone thought it might be safer to find someone who has actually had on-air experience, and has dealt with the realities of live broadcasting, and as we considered that in meetings, several people brought up your name. Roone now wants to see an audition, which will require that you get on a plane and go off to film an interview with a subject we've already chosen for you. Time is of the essence here, so we need you to be available to do this next week, probably Tuesday or Wednesday."

Buck and Kay and Linda, all seated around me at the kitchen counter, were alarmed by the look of shock, even anger, on my face. Clearly something had gone wrong with ABC Sports. For a few seconds I was speechless. What I spat out was a reflex.

"Dick, this is crazy. I got the college football thing off my mind months ago. I'm very excited about program planning, and I'm only about a month from showing up. I'm flattered of course, but this just isn't what I want to do."

Ebersol's voice was calm but insistent. "I'm not sure you heard me right. ROONE wants to see you on camera. He's looking for the right person to get the television chance of a lifetime, and he thinks that might be you. You need to take a step back and think sensibly about this. And you will not lose the program planning job. I give you my personal word of honor we will not give it to anyone else. The whole idea of the college-age reporter thing is that you do it for one season, and every year there will be someone else. You need to get on a plane and go do the audition interview."

Linda's face wore a *don't be crazy* look. Buck and Kay were fascinated, waiting expectantly, as I agreed to do it. Who was the subject and where would I go?

"You're going back to Birmingham. This time you will fly first class.

You are going to sit down and interview a guy named George Mira. He's a quarterback with the Birmingham Americans of the World Football League, and the story is it's his last shot. He's been through the NFL as a high draft choice and the CFL as a celebrated NFL alumnus, and now he's in Birmingham, and your focus is the personal story. You can do this, right? And oh, by the way, Roone is your overall boss for the program planning job here, so there's really only one smart answer."

I was as close to speechless as would ever be possible for me. George Mira? It was as if they had hit the jackpot in a game of pin the tail on the donkey. I worked to maintain my composure as I finished the conversation with Dick and got off the phone. The three faces in the kitchen in Swan Corner were alive with curious expectation. I looked at them and gave it a beat to heighten the effect.

Linda went first. "SO? What's the headline?"

"I'm going to be the college-age reporter. Or one of them anyway, feels like there will be two of us. Me and the Stanford guy."

"He told you, you are being hired?"

"No, not exactly. They want me to do an audition interview. But the universe has already made up its mind, that's clear. They want me to interview George Mira."

Buck and Kay didn't know what that meant, but Linda did. Hanging in our closet, back in Chapel Hill, was a No. 10 University of Miami football jersey, commemorative of my early years as a junior high school nerd living right down the street from the older girl who had just now been told that her 25-year-old husband had been given the network television chance of a lifetime. George Mira, No. 10, was not only my hero from his days starring for the Hurricanes, I also probably knew more about his story than most members of his family.

Along the way I had pursued, first as a platonic friend, then as an unlikely fiancée candidate, the kind of Miami girl I'd never had the courage to even call on the phone in high school. And against the devoted wishes of her father, I had married her and brought her to Chapel Hill where she preceded me into grad school. And now we were only a couple of steps away from both owning master's degrees in media fields and heading off to New York to pursue network jobs.

2

White and Black

Peggy Lampley made Jim watch his first boxing match
(Courtesy of Jim Lampley)

There's an undeniable starting point for my unconscious journey toward the sport of professional boxing, and it begins with the most frequently repeated line in my autobiographical yarns: "My father died when I was five years old."

James Bratton Lampley, a victim of cancer at age 35, was the second of my mother's husbands to die, and the second to leave behind an only son.

My brother's father, Fred Trickey, had perished when the transport plane bringing him back from Saipan at the end of World War II crashed into a mountain near Brevard, North Carolina. One of Fred Trickey's B-29 squadron buddies was Jim Lampley, who at that moment had already arrived back in Hendersonville, 18 miles from where Fred Trickey's flight went down.

A few days later Jim Lampley took a uniform and some medals to Peggy Trickey at MacDill Air Force Base in Tampa, Florida, so she would have something meaningful to put into a casket. Over the next few years, he made increasingly frequent trips to Tampa to continue providing comfort, emotional support, and, eventually, love. Peggy Clark Trickey became Peggy Lampley in 1948, and I was born in 1949. My four-years-older half-brother's name was changed to Fred Lampley.

Our family of four settled in Hendersonville, where my father's war heroism had earned him a Chrysler dealership, prominently situated on Main Street. My father won the golf championship and established a course record of 65 at Hendersonville Country Club. His younger brother, a doctor, began supervising care for my mother, who had suffered rheumatic fever as a teenager and had lingering cardiac maladies as the result.

By Christmas of 1953 my mom was in trouble, and my uncle arranged for her to go to New York for a surgical intervention to prevent heart failure. The experience was scary enough for a New York hospital to allow my father to be checked into the room with her for a full exploratory physical. He had some mysterious discomfort in his abdomen.

On the day before her scheduled surgery, doctors entered the room to deliver unexpected bad news: Jim Lampley had cancer, and it was advanced to the point where the prognosis was troublesome. It was imperative for both of them to know that before she went forward with an open-heart procedure.

But with two young boys waiting back in Hendersonville, there was no rational option. My mom went through her surgery, and it provided a new prognosis for an extended lifespan. My father was not as fortunate. He died at home in Hendersonville on August 1, 1954.

In 1955, about 16 months after my father had died, my mother took me with her to an adult cocktail party in our woodsy mountainside neighborhood and guided me down a hallway to what I recall as a guest bedroom, where a small television set had been placed on a dinner tray.

"Sit here, and you are doing this because if your father were still alive this is exactly what you would be doing with him. You are going to watch a boxing match on a program called the Gillette Friday Night Fights. It's Sugar Ray Robinson versus Bobo Olson for the middleweight championship, and in the next hour or so a man named Don Dunphy is going to tell you a lot of what you need to know about boxing. And, by the way, Sugar Ray Robinson is my favorite fighter. I like the way he moves. He's a dancer in the ring."

In the years to follow, I gradually gathered an understanding of what it meant in 1955 for a white mother in the South to specifically instruct her six-year-old son to appreciate the aesthetic style and talent of a Black fighter. My mother was different from the rest of the adults in the Lampley family who embodied and projected the dominant racial attitudes and instincts of that time and place. But not my mom. And I'll never know where that came from, given that I clearly remember from our very infrequent visits to Memphis to see her parents and other family members that they were just like the Lampleys, meaning no one was taking the trouble to employ a disciplined pronunciation of the word "Negro."

She went further than that. On occasions after leaving some family or neighborhood event, on the way home, my mother would lecture Fred and me: "Just be clear, regardless of what you see and hear, the one attitude you will NEVER display or project is racism. In this household racism is the cardinal sin. We will try in every way to support the movement toward civil rights, to express our belief in equality, and to push back against the ugliness of racism. You will do this because it is the only right thing to do."

Two decades later, I paid special attention to the basketball coach at the University of North Carolina, Dean Smith, when he said, "You shouldn't be proud about doing the right thing, you should just do it."

Again, I don't know where it came from. I looked through all the air force yearbooks to see if there were Black faces in the bomber squadrons, evidence that she may have had Black neighbors at MacDill in Tampa or in Pratt, Kansas, where the transition to B-29s had taken place. But there were none. I looked in her Catholic high school yearbook, and every student and teacher was white. So proud of what Mom was teaching us, so happy that it was fuel for endless arguments with my grandparents about the subject, I gleefully subscribed to everything she said and made sure it was a part of my identity. Never knowing what prompted her to give me that gift, I could not have foreseen at the time how pivotal it would be in the ultimate development of a professional identity.

From 1955, when I first watched a boxing match on television, through 2019, when my somewhat accidental broadcasting career reached its logical end, America's passion for competitive sports played an omnipresent role in the rebalancing of race relations in America. Jackie Robinson and Bill Russell, already breakthrough stars of their professional teams, were two early pioneers. For me, it was also Cassius Clay.

It was the evolution of social consciousness propelled by sports, and it continues to this day. I still marvel to think that my mother was an

16

unlikely prophet, and I her devoted disciple. I was 11 years old when the athlete who would become the most critical fulcrum of all burst into the societal picture. He was in many ways the direct successor to Sugar Ray Robinson.

———

I was devastated to leave behind all the things that made up my childhood in Hendersonville. It was demoralizing having to accept this just two years after Mom had accommodated the school board's demand that my brother Fred and I skip a grade level, to get us back into a sequence where the teachers would actually have the chance to engage us by teaching new things. Apparently, my mother's conversation level had combined with the natural intelligence of her sons to create an untenable distortion, and all the students around us were working to absorb things Fred and I already knew. So in 1958 Mom agreed with Hendersonville schools that Fred would skip the eighth grade and I would skip the fourth. But with the dealership failing, she decided we should move to Florida.

By Christmas of 1960, Mom had completed the process of getting into life insurance sales training and setting up a house rental in Pompano Beach. I was sent to Florida on a train called the Silver Meteor, heartbroken but resigned to whatever would come next.

I needed an escape from the pure hell of being a social misfit, and the vicarious thrilling world of sports was it. I pored over sports sections in the Pompano *Sun-Sentinel* and the *Fort Lauderdale News*. I collected and traded baseball and football cards and made sure I knew from memory all the statistical and biographical information that appeared on the backs of them. I carried a hand-sized transistor radio to school and found ways to listen to New York Yankees baseball games, soon to become obsessively involved in one of the most absorbing stories in baseball history, Roger

Maris and Mickey Mantle pursuing Babe Ruth's single-season home run record: 60.

Spring of '61, summer of '61, autumn of '61 were all devoted hour by hour to news of the home run chase. Like most every fan in New York, and, I gathered, like most every Yankees fan in the country, I was more romantically attached to Mantle and wanted desperately for him to be the one to break the record. And for some of the one-year-older boys in my Pompano Beach Junior High School class, I became a vital source of information. When Mantle or Maris hit a home run, I would know about it, and know the running number, and how many games remained in the season, and how close the magic number of 61 was. When the pendulum swung in late season toward Maris instead of Mantle, I learned a valuable sports fan lesson: you can't always get what you want.

In September, I showed up for eighth grade at South Miami Junior High School.

In the brief period I had spent in Pompano Beach, I had learned from the *Fort Lauderdale News* that *Parade* magazine's choice as the nation's number one high school football player, a running back named Tucker Frederickson, was suiting up at nearby South Broward High School. But because of my mother's move to the southern half of Dade County, where Miami was, I would never see Tucker Frederickson play high school football. I made a point of complaining to her about it, and she promised to make it up to me.

By now I had only been to two college football games, a 56–3 Clemson-Furman debacle, and later, in 1959, Mom and I had ridden more than 200 miles of rural highways from Hendersonville to see my beloved UNC Tar Heels play the traditional season ender at Duke. It was a dreary, rainy day in Durham, only a short drive from Chapel Hill, redeemed by a unexpected one-sided victory that completed a forgettable 5–5 season. The score was 50–0, which I took as powerful reinforcement about where I was ultimately meant by the universe to go to college. I rode home on a 50-to-nothing cloud, dreaming of the day when I might put on one of those pretty Carolina-blue uniforms and help lead the Tar Heels in flat-out gorgeous Kenan Stadium. At only 10, I was still hopelessly naïve to assume I could still be a college athlete.

During his air force years in Tampa, my father had cultivated an interest in the Florida sports environment, an interest he had retained in the nearly nine years he survived after the end of the war. So my mother had made a couple of visits to the Orange Bowl, and she was familiar with the location and the logistics of the stadium. And she liked that the University of Miami Hurricanes played their home games there on Friday nights.

Entering the fall of 1961, there was optimism for coach Andy Gustafson's Hurricanes.

The quarterback was a rising sophomore who had been heavily recruited but had chosen to stay close to home.

On a roster almost entirely populated by Pennsylvanians, George Mira's hometown listing stuck out dramatically: Key West, Florida. At that point, at age 12, I am not sure I could have told you what a "scrambling" quarterback was. Eventually I would learn the paradigm for that identity was Fran Tarkenton, who had finished his eligibility as a Georgia Bulldog and was drafted in spring of that year by the Minnesota Vikings. I would watch Tarkenton and could see the similarity. But to my boyhood eyes it didn't appear Tarkenton was as radical a specimen, as constantly on the edge of disaster, as constantly capable of pulling rabbits out of hats, as George Mira. He wore No. 10, and for me that number now emphatically eclipsed Johnny Unitas's 19.

I was enthralled. My life was now focused on two repeating vicarious thrills: Friday nights at the Orange Bowl and the occasional moment when Cassius Clay would appear on television, boisterously picking a round in which he would use his remarkable combination of speed and balance and technique to banish another hapless, ill-equipped opponent. And as the societal force and momentum of the civil rights movement gathered steam, he used that moment on camera and on microphones to taunt the white establishment my grandparents and aunts and uncles personified.

When my mom and I would climb the ramps of the Orange Bowl to reach our season-ticket seats in the next to last row of the upper deck, the process was maddeningly time consuming due to how often Mom had to stop and struggle desperately to regain her breath. I would get unwarrantedly angry, oblivious as I was to the lifetime challenges of a rheumatic heart condition that had already subjected her to two open-heart surgeries.

My inborn sense of entitlement combined with the brazen declarations of my über authoritative grandmother ("I love all my grandchildren the same, but Jimbo is special") made me impossible for my mother to please. I feel shame looking back at it now. But this was the fall of 1961, and she was trying to get me to accept my life's circumstances. And that was now in the hands of a white college quarterback and a Black boxer, born six days apart in January 1942.

3

Cassius Marcellus Clay

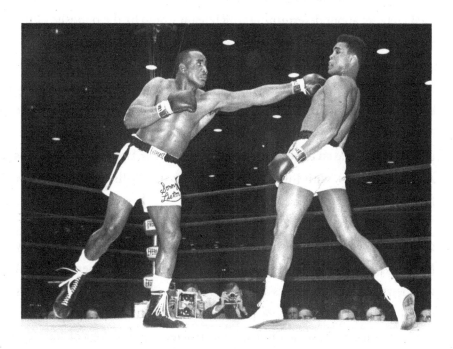

Jim was at Convention Hall as Clay shocked the world
(dpa picture alliance/Alamy Stock Photo)

'll never know how my mother came to believe what she so fervently believed. I only know she is alone in having shaped my attitudes toward politics and society—and therefore the most responsible influence in the worldview that would fuel what became my career. She made me a devoted fan of most sports, and she made me fiercely anti-racist. It's the second part I will never understand.

I not only adopted my mother's thinking on the subject, but in some ways I took it to another level. Early in my education as a baseball fan, I asked my paternal grandfather, James Hoyt Lampley, which was his favorite baseball team. This was around 1959 or so, and he replied he was a Washington Senators fan because owner Calvin Griffith had staunchly declared he would never put a Negro player in a Senators uniform. I immediately set about determining which team would be the opposite of the Senators and committed to the San Francisco Giants as my favorite.

They had Willie Mays, Orlando Cepeda, Leon Wagner, and later Juan Marichal on the roster, all terrific players of color. And I stayed up very late on the night of July 30, 1959, with a transistor radio, listening as Willie McCovey broke into the majors with a 4-for-4 arrival: two singles and two triples. It was heaven to be a Giants fan that summer, right up until the Los Angeles Dodgers, with Junior Gilliam and Maury Wills, edged them out for the pennant.

I sampled the Celtics of Bill Russell and Sam and K. C. Jones. I marveled at the running prowess of Jim Brown even as I rooted for Lenny Moore and the Colts to beat him. And then in the summer of 1960, I watched the Rome Olympics and discovered Cassius Marcellus Clay. I was one of millions.

You couldn't have fictitiously constructed a more logical hero for me. He had style and skills and skin color. He was using the name of a 19th-century Kentucky abolitionist given to his father to taunt the white establishment, even though he mistakenly thought the name came from a slave owner. And his gift for brash gab was otherworldly. To say I fell in love was an understatement. I fell into obsession.

I wanted Cassius Clay to fight for the heavyweight title immediately, as I was vaguely aware an Olympic gold medalist named Pete Rademacher had done exactly that. So it was through the development process Clay pursued under the teaching of trainer Angelo Dundee that I began to learn how boxing careers are carefully built. I watched him get knocked down by Sonny Banks. I could see that the Doug Jones fight was very close and could in the eyes of the judges have easily gone Jones's way. I talked my mother into driving 30 miles from our new home in Miami near the Palmetto Expressway to the 5th Street Gym to watch Dundee train my hero. Twice. I met Dundee briefly, but I never saw him training Clay. I saw him with welterweight Luis Rodríguez and light heavyweight Willie Pastrano instead.

In June 1963, Clay faced off against older, smaller, but hard-punching British star Henry Cooper before an open-air crowd of 35,000 in London's Wembley Stadium. It was a risky way for Clay to make a larger-than-usual sum of money on the way to the now-expected showdown with heavyweight champion Sonny Liston. And in the fourth round, Clay was floored again, this time by Cooper's trademark left hook, before getting up to overwhelm Cooper with speed and force a fifth-round stoppage.

The one left hook with which Cooper had floored Clay ensured that "Enry" never again needed to buy his own ale in Great Britain. It also meant Clay's Louisville brain trust would be loony to wait any longer to deal with Liston. The biggest fight boxing could now make was set for February 25, 1964, in Miami Beach.

The morning *Miami Herald* and the afternoon *Miami News* had boxing reporters, and columnists Edwin Pope and John Crittenden were avid followers, speculating in print that if Sonny Liston vs. Cassius Clay could be pulled off, a likely setting for the fight was the Miami Beach Convention Center. I began generating and hoarding car washing and lawn mowing money to buy a ticket for the fight. I was about as bashful as Cassius Clay regarding my intentions, and several of my neighbors took great glee from taunting me for my naïveté, assuring me Liston would shatter my dreams and Clay's chin. I grew more and more vehement in defense of the Louisville Lip. Grass grew, cars got dirty, and I was closing in.

I was still several lawns and car washes away from affording the ticket, but I would get there. When my mom drove over to Miami Beach to visit the box office, she shelled out a three-figure sum on my behalf. I can't remember now, more than 60 years later, whether it was $100 or $150. I know it was one or the other, and Mom was astonished and amused. She also fully understood that the lessons and values she had taught me about politics and society figured into my need to see the fight. So there was no pushback. If it were today, in the social media and collector culture era, I would surely save the ticket, but looking back, I didn't. Too bad, because it would have been the most cherished investment of my life. But if Liston were to have annihilated Clay, as most pundits expected, the value would be negligible.

I was not yet 15. Mom drove me to the convention center and dropped me off, saying she would track the fight via radio or maybe in a bar and come back to a designated spot near one side of the arena whenever it was over. Given Liston's history, it was understood that might be a matter of just a few minutes. Logic dictated that the longer the event lasted, the more it might favor the younger, taller, faster, more athletic Clay.

But most radio commentary focused on Clay's reported panic attack at the pre-fight medical exam. Reports were that he had an out-of-control heart rate, and legitimate thought was given to calling off the fight. I had no idea what to think of that. Neither did Mom. When I got out of the car, she was adamant that I should not wander away from the arena door after the conclusion, regardless of the outcome.

"Don't you come looking for me. Count on me to find you. We have no idea what this place is going to be like if something unexpected happens tonight."

Later she took credit for her prophecy.

I had forgotten about the concept of the undercard. Luckily my seatmate, a man in his 50s, had a cheat sheet and knew everything. He knew the names and weights of the fighters, knew how they fit into a larger narrative if they did, knew who the clear favorites were and who were the "opponents," a term that seemed redundant to me but which he explained was not.

Somehow, Mom had bought me a good seat for the three-figure price. I had a surprisingly clear view of the ring, not like sitting at the top of the upper deck in the Orange Bowl, where I watched George Mira play quarterback for Miami.

The fight marked a major step forward in my evolution as a sports fan. For three *college* football seasons, 1961 through 1963, my adulation for Mira had been at the emotional center of my vicarious thrill structure, and I had memorized and idolized every statistic, every physical nuance, every salient detail of the Key West–to–Miami Mira narrative. Nothing else competed head-to-head with that at the time.

And it was critical in the ongoing dialogue of my transition from boyhood to adolescence that I adopted Mom's sociopolitical values, not those of the Lampleys in Hendersonville and Memphis. No icon was more central to that piece of the competition than Cassius Clay. So that was part of what was at stake as I settled into the seat for the fight. It was important that he not be embarrassed. In my heart I really believed he was going to win. He would, as he was putting it, "upset the world."

My heart was beating with a level of excitement I'm sure I had never felt. My seatmate was kind and considerate, and he urged me not to get my hopes up, and to understand that Clay was very young and had been rushed into this. My seatmate wasn't elderly, but I thought of 50s as elderly at that time.

I was shocked at the preponderance of boos when Clay entered. How could all these people be so ardently opposed to someone whose ideas were so right, who had won an Olympic gold medal for America, who was fighting against a visibly sinister ex-con? It didn't make sense to me, but I had to some degree been prepared by the laughter of my neighbors in Southwest Miami, especially the men, when I had explained to them the Cassius Clay–based urgency of earning money washing cars and mowing lawns. I considered the possibility some of them had gone along with it just to chuckle when I got my comeuppance.

I realized, more graphically than before, how alone my mother was in the social spectrum of Miami. I had come to South Florida with a vague expectation there would be less overt racism than what I had seen and heard in North Carolina. Then I saw the local map designation for "Central Negro District." Now this. The things my hero was fighting for were more threatening to the white Miami majority than Sonny Liston's rap sheet, which included two years in state prison for armed robbery and larceny. This was indeed the most meaningful moment of my life to this point, and for reasons far beyond athletic competition. This was not football or baseball or basketball. This was the distinctive societal drama of boxing.

From the opening bell forward to the shocking conclusion, it all took less than a half hour. It felt like just a few minutes. In round one Clay was tentative, but it seemed clear to me he was too fast and athletic for Liston to catch up to. In round two Clay gained greater confidence, and my seat-mate, with an air of shock in his voice, said something to the effect he was "starting to put his punches together."

In the third round I got a clearer picture of what "putting his punches together" looked like from a naked-eye view, and suddenly Clay landed a lightning right-hand shot and Liston stepped back, pawed at his left cheek where the stain of blood seemed to emerge, and looked down at his glove in unmistakable shock. My seatmate was speechless. I shouted in exultation a couple of times. More speechlessness.

The fourth round didn't seem to fit with the pattern of round three. By the end of the round Clay, who had been scoring at will in the third, was, in the words of my seatmate, "running like a deer." I couldn't argue the point, and after the round it appeared there was havoc or confusion in Clay's corner. I couldn't imagine what was causing all that. Had Cassius been hit by one of Liston's now-legendary power shots, the kind that had twice obliterated former heavyweight champ Floyd Patterson? If so, I hadn't seen it.

In the fifth round there was more running, I couldn't deny it, and the inevitable Liston knockout victory seemed for a couple of minutes just on the horizon. My heart sank and my voice receded into silence. But by the end of the round Clay was still standing, and Liston seemed to have backed off a bit. My seatmate made a comment to the effect of "Liston looks old. This is not what anyone expected." I couldn't resist brazenly responding with "it's EXACTLY what I expected," which drew a friendly laugh.

The sixth round was a wipeout. Clay was circling elusively but stepping forward and landing sharp combinations. Now Liston really DID look old, a message portrayed by a countenance of discouragement on his face. I was celebrating enough to visibly annoy some of the others sitting around me, but the "elderly" stranger who had now become my friend was smiling and laughing as if to say, *Go right ahead.*

When Cassius stepped out into the ring for round seven, Liston just stayed on his stool. It seemed unreal, and there were many around me who were expressing disbelief. But my seatmate said, "Go ahead and celebrate, kid. You've got what you wanted. Your boy is now the heavyweight champion of the world. He did what almost none of us thought he could do. Go find your mother and have a big night. And tomorrow you can begin telling your neighbors you were right all along."

Going home in the car, shouting and celebrating with Mom, I felt as though I was now living in a markedly different world. The rights and capabilities of aspiring Black people, a cause so emotionally valuable to Mom and me, could never again be credibly disputed. Cassius Clay had wiped all that out before the eyes of the world. We heard all the post-fight summations on the radio and heard the words Clay had shouted at ringside while Liston had skulked off to his dressing room.

When we got home, I climbed onto the roof of our rented tract house and began shouting, "I have upset the world! I am the greatest! I banished the Big Ugly Bear." Pretty soon Mom came out into the front yard, yelling, "Get down off the roof! You are going to get us arrested for disturbing the peace." But she was grinning when she said it. She couldn't deny she was just as exultant as I was.

Two days later Clay announced he was a follower of something called the Nation of Islam, and eventually the nation's leader Elijah Muhammad had given him the name "Muhammad Ali." To say I was thrown for a loop is a dramatic understatement. If my schoolmates and neighbors had fully understood it, the response might have been worse, but really, no one fully understood. It was a language that in February 1964 was largely impenetrable for American culture. Even my mom didn't fully get it, and she was the smartest person I knew. Islam? What was that?

It took weeks, maybe months, to sink in. But eventually I realized he had taught me a lesson: No matter how much I celebrated him, no matter how proprietary I felt about him, his identity was all his, not mine. That was a necessary step toward emotional maturity about sports.

The following year, upon learning his local draft board had changed his status from conscientious objector to eligible for mandatory military service, Ali instantaneously informed my attitude toward the war in Vietnam with what became a famous quote: "I ain't got no quarrel with them Vietcong."

My brother and I were the sons of legitimate World War II heroes. But neither of us could fathom why we should risk our lives in Vietnam. And Mom was even more adamant: "You'll go to Canada before you will be a part of that."

4

Magic Man

"Dad, who was that man?" (Courtesy of Jim Lampley)

When I was turning 14 and started watching network news, Mom liked Chet Huntley and David Brinkley on NBC. Brinkley was from Wilmington, North Carolina, and had a matter-of-fact style with a flat, almost monotone delivery. Huntley seemed more sophisticated and, as Mom put it, "more New York." I scouted around a bit and settled on my own preference for Walter Cronkite on CBS, having watched several of the Mercury project space launches in school, and it just seemed that Cronkite and the people around him knew more and cared more about whether the United States would beat the Russians in explorations of outer space. CBS was to me more spirited on the coverage of civil rights, too, and there was something about the cadence with which Cronkite would say the name "Martin Luther King." There was reverence in it.

Early on the afternoon of Friday, November 22, 1963, I had finished my Phys Ed class, quickly showered, and arrived at the outset of geometry on the second floor of Southwest Miami Senior High School. The teacher was a very young, very cool, very popular guy named John Tracy. He had the occasional capacity to make the subject interesting and was utterly unafraid to reach across the invisible barrier to touch the minds of adolescents who were closing in, however awkwardly and unconsciously, on chronological adulthood.

As we sat down, about 25 of us, he instructed everyone to close our math books and sit still. Something had happened in Dallas, and we would listen to the radio news. The rest is a blur leading to our early dismissal with a stipulation, probably mostly ignored, that we should go straight home. I walked there, a quiet 45 minutes, and turned on the television to find Walter Cronkite at the news desk in shirtsleeves. The events weren't real to my 14-year-old mind until I saw him validate the details of what happened, summarizing with critical detail that the president was dead, and then taking off his glasses.

I sat there in a daze until Mom walked in, and the next three days became a graphic, unforgettable enactment of her critical role as my ad hoc civics teacher, history tutor, moral conscience, and cultural guide. There seemed to be nothing about this that she didn't know, no nuance about which she did not have strong feelings, very few moments when she couldn't predict what Cronkite or his reporters would say next.

Having sat through most of World War II on air force bases waiting for news that was all too elusive, now the details of JFK's assassination were immediate and tangible, and she passionately captioned them all for me: the bloodstains on Jackie Kennedy's pink skirt, the sudden and inexplicable shooting of Lee Harvey Oswald in the Dallas Police Department basement, the riderless horse and two beautiful children standing at the edge of Pennsylvania Avenue, the coffin lying in state in the Capitol rotunda. Mom had seen the moment when Cronkite paused, removed his glasses, wiped his eyes. She described the piercing humanity of it, and I understood why she was so moved.

By Saturday or Sunday, I was asking her what might be most affected in our lives by this, and she made clear her most salient concern was the civil rights movement. The president and Attorney General Bobby Kennedy—his brother—had been aggressive and fearless in pushing for school integration in the South, and the issue was central to Mom's concept of what would constitute a morally responsible society. Lyndon Johnson was a Southerner from Texas who had the opposite record for much of his time in Congress, though he helped pass a civil rights bill when he was Senate majority leader in the 1950s. She suspected the assassination had something to do with the civil rights movement, and she would lose sleep over that. She was thinking of her life insurance clients in the ghetto neighborhoods of Miami, not far from where she had moved us to have it better than the rural North Carolina she had outgrown.

———

Fifteen months after the first fight in Miami Beach, Sonny Liston got his rematch title shot against the heavyweight champion variously identified in American newspapers as Muhammad Ali, Cassius X, and Cassius Clay. There was still no shortage of detractors who either didn't want to believe or didn't want to honor that this controversial would-be "draft dodger" had legitimately won the biggest prize in competitive sports.

The fight was originally set for Boston. A few months before the first scheduled date, Ali's fellow Nation of Islam follower Malcolm X was assassinated by gunshot, a stark sign of violent tumult in the Black Muslim world. A decision was made to take the event out of Boston, and it landed in an obscure arena in the rural mill town of Lewiston, Maine.

Mom paid for me to get into a movie theater showing the live fight in South Miami. Midway into the first round, Muhammad Ali landed a short right-hand countering over Liston's jab in the center of the ring. It didn't fit my concept of a classic knockout shot, but it was clear to me the punch *did* land on Liston's cheek. He went down and stayed down and that was it.

The debate was feverish: Was it a real power punch? Did the aging Liston take a dive? Was it a fix? Was Liston so spooked by the fear that bullets of revenge for Malcolm X were going to fly that night that he took the safe way out? There was a lot to discuss, but indisputably Liston was done, and the king of the boxing world was the Louisville Lip.

At my household in Miami that discussion rapidly gave way to more and more anxiety about the escalating War in Vietnam. My older brother, Fred, owned an automatic exemption from the draft because his father had died in active duty coming back home from Saipan. But I was theoretically eligible for the draft and now less than two years from age 18.

And my instinct was to trust my mom's judgment, and also the judgment of Muhammad Ali. And in June 1966 I would be graduating from high school and heading off to college. There was only one place I really wanted to go next, and that was to Chapel Hill.

Suffering through Ali's three-year exile from the ring was excruciating. Anticipating his return was rejuvenating. Devoid of money to access the closed-circuit showing, I received the news of Joe Frazier's victory with grief on March 8, 1971. I was hoping that when I watched a delayed telecast that weekend, it would show me the judges had it wrong in their unanimous decision. But that wasn't what I saw.

From there forward were more disappointments, like the surprise split-decision loss to Ken Norton in San Diego, and moments of extreme exultation, like the rope-a-dope knockout of George Foreman in the Rumble in the Jungle. But virtually no boxing careers end happily, and Ali's was in every way the prime example of the experience.

On an October night in 1980, Ali met his former sparring partner and mentee Larry Holmes for the title that now belonged to the former understudy, the two of them acting out a rite of passage as old and familiar as the sport itself. No serious student of the sport would have deluded himself into believing the aging global icon still had any chance to win the fight. Even I didn't really indulge in that fantasy.

By now I was an established figure at ABC Sports, and by invitation I watched in a private suite at 1330 Sixth Avenue, where Roone Arledge hosted a gathering of New York glitterati for the closed-circuit feed. By about round 9 or 10, as Holmes's systematic beatdown of the older, tired fighter was getting unbearable to watch, I was suddenly treated to the single greatest line of boxing commentary I have ever heard, even despite all the years I spent calling fights with Larry Merchant and George Foreman and Max Kellerman and others of their ilk. It came from a seemingly unlikely source.

Standing near a monitor, eyes glued to the screen in anticipation of the poignant stoppage, I felt a friendly poke just below my rib cage on the right side of my body. I looked over at Mick Jagger, whose acquaintance I had made four years earlier at the Montreal Olympics. He leaned toward me.

"Lamps, do you know what we are watching?"

"No, Mick. What are we watching?"

"It's the end of our youth."

To this day, it gives me chills. And it cannot be topped. It just can't.

When you grow up from childhood into adulthood with an idol like Ali, the last thing you expect is that you will someday meet that man, talk to that man about his game and his life, truly befriend him, and learn from him as though he is your intended universal instructor. That happened to me. I can only describe it in those most simple and direct terms. There is no other experience quite like it.

In the spring of 1991, I was master of ceremonies at the annual dinner of the Boxing Writers Association of America at a midtown New York hotel. The dinner was taking place simultaneously with the publication of the most intimate and thorough of all Ali biographies, Thomas Hauser's simply titled *Muhammad Ali*. As a plausible promotion for the dinner and the book, the boxing writers prevailed upon Muhammad to autograph copies in the hotel lobby. He sat down and began doing it in the afternoon, then was brought into the greenroom to relax and refresh before signing more books and delivering a keynote speech that night.

I was in that greenroom with my 10-year-old daughter, Brooke, whom I had promised to bring to the dinner. But now I needed to go out into Manhattan traffic to run a series of errands, and it would be more challenging if I took her along. I asked her if she might be comfortable staying and waiting for me in the greenroom. She was already used to that kind of thing, so I began looking around for a likely choice to chaperone her, and predictably Ali spoke up.

"I'll watch over her. Take all the time you need, just leave her with me."

As I went out the door, I glanced back to see him taking a deck of cards out of a briefcase. Magic tricks. I had heard about that for years.

That night Ali signed hundreds of books. He was right next to me on the dais, and Brooke was out in the audience seated at the HBO Sports table with a group of people she barely knew. There was a lengthy list of award presentations, each with a recipient speech. Ali was scheduled to close the show. As soon as dinner was complete and the waiters were clearing tables and the dais, I looked over and saw that Muhammad was verging toward sleep. And out in front of me at the HBO table, I could see my daughter was bored, cranky, and spent. I could conjure only one solution.

Calling on my de facto authority as master of this ceremony, I motioned Brooke to climb the stairs up to the dais and sit in my seat. Instantly Muhammad revived, and a whole new set of magic tricks began, these all involving silverware and napkins and dinner programs.

Brooke was beyond enthralled, and at the end of a long night, Ali stood up and successfully negotiated the speech. It was like a movie scene.

In the taxi, taking Brooke back uptown to her mother's Madison Avenue apartment, she turned to me in the darkness of the back seat and portrayed real curiosity.

"Dad, who was that man?"

"Well, that is a big answer and someday you will surely know it all. But I'll just start with this: he's probably the most famous man in the world."

I sat with my arm around her and quietly fought back tears. Tears of pride, tears of unaccountable fortune for me and my daughter, tears for the imminent loss prefigured by the 49-year-old Ali's advancing Parkinson's syndrome. Tears I couldn't let her see on that precious night.

Ten years later Brooke graduated number one among 66 in the class of 1998 at the American School of London. For the graduation program, each student was asked to choose a couplet of poetry to define himself or herself, something many of them would surely keep as a reminder of that beachhead of accomplishment. Not surprisingly, selections from Lord Byron and Elizabeth Barrett Browning and Robert Frost were popular. I had flown from Los Angeles to London to be there for the ceremony, and there in the program was my prized daughter's selection.

Brooke Lampley, valedictorian

"Float like a butterfly. Sting like a bee."

By Muhammad Ali.

5

First Meetings

When ABC Sports president Roone Arledge made a last-minute decision in August 1974 to hire me as part of his revolutionary new college football sideline scheme, neither he nor his lieutenants knew the one identity element I had been holding back from them for months.

But at some point, closer to the start of the season, I was summoned to New York to sit with a financial officer (as the producers invariably called him, a "green eyeshade") and learn how to use an air travel card, how to treat the daily cash per diem, how to fill out and properly compute an expense report, which card to use to check into hotels, etc. He went through about 20 minutes of this before sitting back in his chair, smiling, and saying, "Anything else you are curious about?"

His name was Bob Apter, and executive producer Chuck Howard had explained to me that Apter was the number two financial officer at ABC Sports, but there was no reason for me to meet his superior, so for anything administrative he was my guy.

Now or never. "Yeah, thanks. I am about to go on national television with a yellow blazer and an ABC Sports identity, and I haven't yet been introduced to Roone Arledge. Should I be surprised by that?"

Apter burst out laughing. "Oh, hell no. There's nothing surprising about that. We've got people who have worked here for years and haven't met Roone Arledge. He's a virtual recluse, almost never comes to work in the daytime, and if you ever meet him casually, it will probably be in the restroom. That's where I first met him, and I had already been here two years."

Bob's office was on the 16th floor at 1330 Avenue of the Americas. That was the ancillary floor for the sports division. All the royalty were on the 28th floor, and because of the overwhelming success the division had achieved under Arledge, several of them already had hall-of-fame resumes even while still in their 20s and 30s.

So there was an aura about the 28th floor, and I felt it. Now that my business with Bob Apter was done and I had no further official agenda in the building, it was thrilling to me that I needed to go back to 28, where all the LeRoy Neiman paintings lined the walls, the glamorously Italian receptionist Phyllis Colonna smiled from behind the front desk, and after retrieving my suitcase I could hit a restroom before grabbing a cab in afternoon traffic for LaGuardia.

I left the suitcase with Phyllis and walked into the men's room. And there at the bank of washbasins, having just exited a stall, was the unmistakable physical presence of the guy they called "the Redhead."

Roone Arledge, no doubt. He could never have imagined that my first quiet thought was: *Wow, he looks a lot like his dad.*

What I had never said to anyone (because how exactly would it have come up?) was that somewhere in my Hendersonville, North Carolina, childhood I had heard his credit on a telecast and asked my mom, "Do you think he is related to our neighbor Roone Arledge?" And she told me, "Yes, he is their son." All through my teenage summers I had made money caddying at Hendersonville Country Club, and "Mr. Arledge" was an occasional client. I was aware that the Arledges had retired to our Blue Ridge mountains from New York. Mrs. Arledge was in my mother's bridge club.

So after the initial greetings and his warm welcome to the network, I jumped right into "By the way, how's your father?"

A look of shocked curiosity. A confused grin. "Well, why in the world would you be asking me that?"

I explained about the caddying. I don't think I even got to the bridge club.

He held out a hand to terminate the conversation. "Listen, I've got to run. It is really great to meet you, and you're going to do great things for us. But by all means don't EVER tell anyone that. NEVER. Are we clear on that?"

Of course we were. A sworn secret. How would they have explained that out of 432 candidates, they had wound up putting on the air the only one who had caddied for Roone Arledge's father fewer than 10 years before? They wouldn't have to. I'd be the last person alive to reveal something that compromising.

Ever.

———

As that first ABC Sports college football season on the sidelines developed, Arledge's highest-ranking production lieutenant, Chuck Howard, became my mentor. The established staples of the division's programming prior to the 1971 inauguration of *Monday Night Football* had been college football and *Wide World of Sports*, and as the senior VP of production, Howard assigned himself the featured games in the fall and the mainstream Olympics sports events like track and field and swimming through the rest of the year. He also produced golf.

But in September 1974, I was concerned mainly about the sideline and how to create story material in a highly restricted space. I didn't realize at first Chuck was thinking about that when he advised me to begin finding reasons to travel to Tuscaloosa and Austin, and to try to promote face-to-face contact with two coaches I already idolized and cheered for, Bear Bryant and Darrell Royal.

Back in Chapel Hill, I flew to Birmingham and rented a car to drive down to Tuscaloosa. Chuck had reached out to make me an introductory appointment with Bryant, and step one was to try to beat the great man to his office on Monday morning, which required getting up before dawn. I was carefully instructed that to be later than Bear would be disrespectful, so I was seated in his outer office, facing his secretary, when he arrived, sometime before seven. We began chatting, he asked me personal questions about my small-town background in the Blue Ridge, and sometime before eight I watched in quiet astonishment as the secretary brought in a Crimson mug with the Alabama *A*, and Bear casually opened a bottom desk drawer, pulled out a pint of Smirnoff vodka, and liberally enhanced his black coffee.

Later I was told that was the highest compliment he could have paid me. An even higher compliment, I was assured, than when we went onto the practice field for Monday morning drills and he allowed me up on the top deck of his famous observation tower, where I watched as he showed off his capacity for minutely detailed observations, all shouted out through a megaphone.

"Hey, tell the strong-side tackle to turn his outside foot toward the boundary at a forty-five degree angle in his stance. That way he'll beat the running back to the corner!" An order tossed out from 40 yards away.

Bryant was an instant friend, maybe because I was a Southern boy whose mother had struggled to raise me. During my first season when some veteran Southern sports editors tried to deep-six the entire sideline experiment, Bear backed me and ABC for the innovation.

Royal was a little pricklier when, by mid-October, we were in Austin for an Arkansas-Texas game that felt like it was scheduled way too early.

On the third weekend of the season, Texas had lost to Texas Tech in Lubbock when a hot quarterback named Tommy Duniven scorched the Longhorns' secondary in a 26–3 Red Raiders upset victory.

The loss to Texas Tech took place at a moment of undercurrent in Royal's program. The star of the preceding season was a power runner named Roosevelt Leaks, who had rolled up more than a thousand rushing yards and been chosen as the Southwest Conference Player of the Year. Leaks was back, but now there was competition for his starting role, because Texas had won a once-in-a-lifetime recruiting war with Oklahoma to sign a freshman star named Earl Campbell. Leaks was a bit dinged up with a damaged knee. Campbell was healthier than the proverbial horse. Neither was a blocking back, they both needed to carry the ball, and the entire Texas fan base was watching and debating when the moment would arrive that Campbell replaced Leaks. It was a massive distraction.

Now in the wake of losing in Lubbock, Royal was plotting toward the moment he knew his team needed, though it was a moment that would fly in the face of requisite loyalty to a noble warrior who had shown no slippage. Leaks was still Leaks; he hadn't exactly slipped. But Darrell knew Campbell was cosmic. He needed a way to showcase that for the media and fan base against Arkansas.

I was still reciting memories from the 1969 "Game of the Century" and James Street's game-breaking 44-yard fourth-down pass to Randy Peschel in a game that pitted unbeaten, No. 1 Texas against unbeaten, No. 2 Arkansas. The pass, which came in the waning minutes of the regular-season finale, led to a touchdown. Final score: Texas 15, Arkansas 14.

I was stunned that this time the Horns were playing the Razorbacks before November had even arrived. But now here I was in Austin, meeting Street and drinking Lone Stars with him Wednesday night, and then eating Mexican breakfast Thursday with Royal at Cisco's Bakery & Bar, listening to the coach's speculation about how to showcase Earl Campbell in the right way.

The project would begin with a sit-down interview I was to conduct with Campbell the following morning, an appointment Royal had delegated to legendary publicist Jones Ramsey, and the first time Earl would be speaking in front of a camera. Royal and Ramsey were sure I would be supportive rather than challenging. Producer Terry Jastrow, a Midland, Texas, native and Houston golf graduate, took it to another level. He stopped the camera several times to tell Earl what he wanted him to say and how to say it. I was blown away, and at one point complained to Terry that it was inappropriate to do that. Terry just looked at me and said, "Jim, it's sports, not news, and we don't want to be here all day." For that moment in the evolution of the medium, I'm going to say he was right.

Earl was monosyllabic but unscathed. The following day Leaks was again in the starting lineup, and Campbell waited on the sideline while fans trained binoculars on his number 20 jersey. Fewer than two minutes remained in the first half when a Longhorns student manager showed up at my elbow and said, with considerable urgency, "Coach Royal wants to see you."

The rule I had been quoted by Chuck Howard said not to go within the 35-yard lines, which meant I was barred from in-game contact with players and coaches. I knew of no variation for a head coach who wanted to violate that. But this was Darrell Royal, and I had ardently rooted for him to win national championships, and supposedly he wanted to see me. *Right now.*

Arkansas was in possession of the ball, somewhere near its own 40, and facing a lengthy third-down play when I reached Royal's side. Chewing a blade of grass, he half turned toward me and said, "Let's see if we can set this up." I wasn't sure what he meant.

The third-down Razorbacks pass was incomplete, and as his punt return unit ran onto the field, Royal turned fully toward me and grabbed my shoulders to focus my vision.

"You see number 20, right there? Now watch Earl block this punt."

Campbell was positioning in the center of the line, a couple of feet off the Arkansas center's nose. When the snap sailed back to the punter, Earl exploded past the center and crashed into the punter a split second behind the ball. The punt was engulfed, setting up a Texas touchdown before the half. The crowd buzzed for the rest of the day, as a new era in Longhorns football had begun. Three years later, Campbell won the Heisman Trophy.

That night after a Texas barbecue feast, I witnessed the most majestic of all illustrations of Darrell Royal's godlike power in Austin. Along with Jastrow and a couple of other ABC types, I was allowed into the coach's private postgame gathering in an upstairs suite at the Stephen F Austin Hotel.

Several of Royal's musician friends performed an acoustic concert there, trading the stage back and forth among themselves throughout the evening. They included Willie Nelson, Jerry Jeff Walker, Tracy Nelson, and others from the Old Pecan Street scene. I was fortunate that someone explained to me Royal's house rule for this: Whenever someone was singing, out of respect and attentiveness, not a single person was allowed to utter a word. Not a syllable. Not a whisper. And anyone who did so would immediately be escorted out of the room. No questions asked.

6

Miracle on Snow

Klammer's downhill on Patscherkofel lives on
(SPP Sport Press Photo/Alamy Stock Photo)

t's focal to describe what it was like to witness a downhill ski race in 1976. There's a video screen at the bottom of the mountain next to the finish line, but only a few hundred privileged spectators are situated close enough to benefit from it. For most of those who have shown up to drink in the communion of the experience, watching the downhill is comprised of catching momentary glimpses of each skier slicing by at searing, explosive velocity, then waiting to hear the character of the crowd response at the finish area, where a mounted clock provides the only narrative evidence material to the drama.

As a spectator on the hill in 1976 you didn't watch a ski race, you *felt* it.

This is a story about the greatest downhill in ski racing history and the feelings it engenders, even to this day. And the story is told by the ultimate uninitiated observer, a rookie broadcaster covering his first ski race, at his first of what would become 14 Olympic Games, amid his first trip to Europe just a couple of weeks after his first ill-fated attempts to ski. Seldom have the sublime and the ridiculous collided more propitiously.

In 1974 I experienced a work opportunity that amounted to the functional equivalent of winning a lottery, long before lotteries were coin of the realm in the United States. After an aimless and near-terminally indifferent undergraduate career at the University of North Carolina, and a following year spent writing nondescript publicity releases for an upstart repertory theater company and a doomed-from-the-beginning US Senate campaign, I had stumbled into a series of sports radio niches in Chapel Hill.

Through the luck of meeting some of the right people at the right time, and the willingness to work for $25 a show, I spent a lot of 1972 and 1973 doing pregame and postgame shows for the UNC football and basketball radio networks, interviewing Bill Dooley and Dean Smith constantly and repeatedly, and driving off to little towns I had never seen to describe Chapel Hill High School football to a tiny handful of listeners. My face was still anonymous, but my name became known and, stuck for an answer as to any meaningful career ambition, I used my newfound notoriety to talk my way into a master's degree program in UNC's Department of

Radio, Television, and Motion Pictures. I had no real goal yet, but I had a platform of sorts, and after a near-total failure in undergraduate school, I was beginning to get the impression luck was on my side.

It was. In 1974, capitalizing on technological advances that had emerged from improvised coverage of the kidnapping of nine and the murder of two Israeli athletes at the 1972 Munich Olympics, ABC Sports developed a plan to put a college-age reporter on the sidelines of its college football telecasts with a camera and a microphone.

Throughout its history, sports television has been determined to breach frontiers and get viewers closer to the athletes and the action. This was something new, and after a lengthy public selection process, the network was impressed enough by two candidates to put them on the air, the brilliant Stanford undergraduate Don Tollefson, and the other, a more difficult choice because I was 25 and not technically college age. At the end of the 1974 season Don went off to local television in Philadelphia, and I was invited to stay with the network. To do another season on the sidelines. To begin getting my feet wet on esoteric *Wide World of Sports* shows like the World Lumberjack Championships and the Oriental World of Self-Defense. And in February 1976, in what I saw as the greatest privilege of my life to that date, to be a feature reporter at the Winter Olympic Games in Innsbruck, Austria.

I had never been to Europe. I didn't realize until I landed in Munich that Innsbruck was less than a hundred miles down the road from the scene of the crime that had disrupted the last Olympics three and a half years before. And I arrived in one of the world's most international cities, where, as the games got underway, fans rolled in waving flags, by carloads and buses from nearby countries with winter sports traditions: West Germany, Italy, East Germany, Czechoslovakia, Italy, and Austria's more glamorous next-door neighbor, Switzerland.

There are some American sports rivalries whose easily identifiable cultural roots will always sing to any sports fan: Alabama vs. Auburn, Michigan vs. Ohio State, the Packers and the Bears, the Celtics and the Lakers. In the world of alpine skiing, that's Austria and Switzerland. Children grow up skiing to school and dreaming of wearing their national colors in Olympic and World Cup competitions. And even in the '70s, when such heroes were ostensibly governed by the archaic code of amateurism the Olympics were still pretending to enforce, they dreamed of the almost limitless money and privilege accrued by the most talented among them.

In the middle of that decade, there were few professional athletes in the world whose bank accounts were more richly stocked than those of so-called amateur ski stars from Austria and Switzerland. Their names and faces were attached to a constant stream of income from ski manufacturers, boot makers, high-end ski clothiers, and expensive accessories like goggles and poles and sunscreens and gloves. Their successes sold resort packages and lift tickets and airfares and the world's best cars and watches. Their nations were constantly locked in economic warfare, and the skiers were the soldiers and the weaponry in those wars.

The 1976 Olympic downhill race, on a slippery mountain in Innsbruck named Patscherkofel, promised the ultimate confrontation between the two global superpowers of skiing. All logic dictated that only two men had a chance to win that gold medal; one was the elegant Swiss World Cup overall champion, and the other was the ultimate Austrian downhiller. As dawn broke over Innsbruck on February 5, 1976, their names were already being shouted through the streets of town. Bernhard Russi. Franz Klammer. Russi. Klammer. But with Austrians outnumbering the opposition, through the morning the chant became louder, ultimately deafening, as nearly 70,000 people gathered on the snowy mountainside, mostly to shout themselves hoarse repeating one word over and over. Klammer, Klammer, Klammer, at once a mantra and a demand, an expression of Austrian birthright and a sacred ritual. Klammer. No other thought mattered.

To say the Austrian farm boy was at that moment the world's best downhiller was a massive understatement. In a sport where winning two or three races a year is a rare success, Klammer had at one point in 1975 won eight of nine World Cup downhills, and in 1976 he had won three in a row coming to the Olympics. Bernhard Russi, from Switzerland, was a stylist, capable of being dominant in slalom and giant slalom, and clearly Klammer's primary competition in the downhill. But Klammer was Mike Tyson or Tiger Woods or Roger Federer at his peak. It would take some unusual stroke of bad luck to seriously compromise his chance of winning. And on the day before the race, that stroke of bad luck arrived.

The order of competition for the Olympic downhill is somewhat based on World Cup rankings. The 15 highest-ranking downhillers on the World Cup circuit see their names tossed into a basket and then drawn out one by one. Everyone else in the field follows in the order of their rank, but logic dictates the winner would emerge from the top 15. And because every run affects the course, softening the snow on the preferred line, the earlier you hit the starter shack the better your chance to ski fast. You want a low number in the draw, and that good fortune fell to Russi, who drew number three. With a whole nation obsessing about him, Klammer drew snake eyes: number 15. And when he awoke to see bright sunlight and unusually warm weather, he saw it was even worse than he had thought. If Russi skied well, the gold medal would likely be out of reach, no matter how many voices thundered Klammer's name.

The race was an instant legend. Russi indeed skied well, and as the snow along the preferred line melted, his time looked more and more impregnable. A helpless Klammer waited in the warming shack and watched as the competition slipped further and further off Russi's temporal mark. Finally, as Klammer walked to the starting shack in a gleaming yellow one-piece, listening to his countrymen pleading for a miracle, he made a fateful decision: On a mountain he knew better than any other World Cup skier, the only chance to win would be to ski the wrong line. He would go where he knew he wasn't supposed to go and hope that if he could somehow hang on for a minute 45 seconds, he might find enough fresh snow to build speed. It might get him killed, but it would be the only way to win. The starting gate opened, and he planted his poles and pushed.

If you've seen the ABC Sports coverage, you're not likely to ever forget it. I had the privilege of watching it all inside the ABC production truck. Announcers Frank Gifford and Bob Beattie are shouting all over each other, desperately trying to portray something that is at once insanely dangerous and spectacularly held together. At one point, Klammer is so far offline he has to swerve to avoid the hay bales lining the edge of the course. At another his left leg is so wildly akimbo that his ski appears to touch his shoulder. And at the first two intermediate timing points he is well behind Russi's marks, but at the third and last one he is only two-hundredths of a second off.

Then the glide to the finish, with his incomparably powerful thighs and buttock muscles deepening into the world's best aerodynamic crouch. The whip turn, the cold stare to the clock, and victory. Ecstasy. A roar you can imagine shaking all of Central Europe. There was never another ski run like it, before or since. And few events, if any, have ever shaken the economies of two neighboring nations the way Franz Klammer did in 105 seconds. A victory for Fischer skis, not Kneissl; for Nordica boots, not Salomon; and for the vacation package at Kitzbuhel, not St. Moritz. No athlete up to that moment had ever so effectively stared down economic pressure as Franz Klammer did on Patscherkofel. The fact he did it as a so-called amateur was a mark of how necessary it had become for the Olympics to transfer into the real world, and in the decades that followed, they did.

Downhillers don't last long at their peaks. Their sport is extremely demanding, and their bodies break down. Klammer had a few more good years, but he was never again as dominant as he was in 1975 and 1976. He was touched by the dark side of the downhill's flirtation with danger when a younger brother suffered a debilitating spinal cord injury while training with the national team. But more than any other competitive skier, Klammer is immortal, and YouTube will surely keep him that way. With an entire nation on his back, he faced up to an impossible task by improvising an impossible plan, and against all odds made it work. As much as any Olympian ever, Franz Klammer is the stuff that dreams are made of. And sometimes in my own dreams, I can still hear 70,000 people rhythmically chanting his name: Klammer. Klammer. Klammer.

7

New York Calling

When I learned in August 1974 that I had been chosen to be the first television reporter to walk onto a college football sideline with a battery pack strapped around my waist, a microphone in my hand, and cameras aligned to take my picture, I instantly foresaw a big change in my life: I was about to earn money. Not the $25 a game the UNC football and basketball radio network had been paying me to do pregame and postgame shows, nor the $100 a game an independent TV provider, UPI Television News, was paying me to do one-minute capsule reports on football and basketball games. That money had been foremost for a while. Now, even though I didn't yet know exactly what I would be paid by ABC Sports, I was pretty sure those previous numbers had been chicken feed.

I picked a Chapel Hill attorney with connections to the UNC football program, and he negotiated via telephone with another green eyeshade in New York. I don't remember now what the initial terms were—maybe $1,000 a game, maybe $1,500—but the following year I was told that we had been "skinned," and the staff employees on the 16th floor had been giggling about it.

But at that moment, my wife, Linda, and I were still living in a $150-a-month apartment in Chapel Hill, and the money I was earning from four or five games a month on ABC dwarfed anything either of us had ever experienced. Linda was able to quit her on-campus secretarial job and enroll in a master's in journalism program. It was the perfect payback for all she had done to help me rescue my checkered academic career. And it would keep her valuably occupied as my travel schedule began to add dates.

The sideline reporter gig had been unequivocally presented as a one-season-only experience. Shortly after an angry confrontation in Chuck Howard's office, the self-assured Duke graduate made clear to me that plan had changed, and there would be no follow-up sideline reporter talent hunt to choose a successor. I was headed to another year on the sidelines.

"You are going to be on national television from every college sideline in the country, recognized in every bar and restaurant the moment you walk in . . . and making a hell of a lot more than $15,000 a month. Don't be stupid."

When my running mate Don Tollefson was moved to one of the nation's most successful major-market local news operations, WPVI-TV in Philadelphia, to continue his development as a sports reporter, it looked on the surface as though Don had lost a contest.

That wasn't really true due to other factors unseen by the public. I was better equipped than Don to curry favor with Chuck Howard, the dictatorial college football producer. You might say it was a Duke-Carolina thing. You might say that because it was. So Don was on the air every night in Philly, and I began a different kind of apprenticeship, handling what amounted to sweat equity for every play-by-play commentator on the staff: *ABC's Wide World of Sports*.

Ninety percent of *Wide World*'s events in the middle '70s were filmed or taped, then edited for broadcast on the first sports anthology show of its kind. An overwhelming majority of habitual television sports viewers in America could recite from memory Jim McKay's opening soliloquy, "Spanning the globe to bring you the constant variety of sport, the thrill of victory, the agony of defeat, the human drama of athletic competition."

And a lot of what was included in "the constant variety of sport" were folk events previously unseen. In the hands of *Wide World*, they became stock items in the repertoire of sports anthologies for decades to come: the wrist wrestling, the lumberjacks, the demolition derby, motorcycles on ice, ski flying, and various other events you might not have been aware of unless you lived in or near one of the exotically anti-exotic locations in which they took place.

For wrist wrestling, Petaluma, California, was also identifiable as the "chicken farming capital of the world"—or egg capital.

For the lumberjacks, the northern Wisconsin buzz-saw town of Hayward. The demolition derby was in Islip, pretty much the geographic center of Long Island's South Shore. Ski flying was a chance to see and learn about Slovenia, at that time 44 years ago not yet the origin point for global basketball prodigy Luka Dončić, but rather a largely unobserved mountainous region of Yugoslavia.

In those days, major airlines didn't have mileage bonus programs. Too bad, because in the vanishing wake of my childhood motion sickness–bred fear of flying, I was now logging as much travel as anyone else in ABC's most travel-prolific division. In the fall there were college football games every Saturday and occasionally on Monday nights. I remained on the sidelines for three impatient years. And as soon as the Sugar Bowl score was final, I was off to service my burgeoning *Wide World* schedule, which I later realized was specific to the continuing evolution of ABC Sports.

For men like Jim McKay, Chris Schenkel, Bill Flemming, Frank

Gifford, and Keith Jackson, all surefire Hall of Fame broadcasters who had visible prestige on the network, it was somewhere between a noble responsibility and a massive pain in the ass to look at the monthly assignment sheet and see that it was your turn again to go to Petaluma or Hayward and suffer through a weekend that now felt like an indignity.

But I soon was made aware that my work on those telecasts was a hit, and a potentially lucrative industry was appearing on the road that lay before me. All the top guys had traded those assignments around among themselves for years, resigning themselves to duty at first, then sooner or later grinding their teeth and sharing their chagrin with their agents. Now there was a new guinea pig in town, and his name was "the kid on the sideline," and for the first time, someone would shoulder the on-air grunt work of covering all that funky stuff repeatedly, year after year.

In very short order, I was privately advised by Chuck Howard, now my professional "Godfather," to offload my Chapel Hill attorney, hook up with a powerful IMG agent named Barry Frank, and negotiate a new contract that would boost my income into the six-figure range. Incredible for me at the time. The phone call to my attorney in Chapel Hill was open and shut, and by early 1978 I was beginning to experience the benefits. I got a real contract with significantly higher per-show fees matched against an underlying annual guarantee. At 28 going on 29, I was earning six figures per year, with the promise of larger numbers down the road if I could continue to please Chuck and his boss Roone Arledge.

Thus, when Linda completed her master's degree at UNC in summer of 1976, it was time to leave Chapel Hill and move to New York.

———

Two years before, when all I had known of New York was 1330 Sixth Avenue and the Warwick Hotel across the street, the idea of that would have been intimidating. Now I was in a different frame of mind. I was pretty sure I was on the verge of becoming a star.

After all, it was the Big Apple. Everyone you met had big dreams. And for now, the pursuit of my big dreams would require repeated trips to places like Petaluma and Hayward, and marathon voice-over sessions in the basement of the ABC Sports and News production factory to call all the action as though it was live. More of an acting job, and I had enthusiasm. Those were the dues that had to be paid for me to begin climbing the ladder at ABC Sports.

The upper tier of the announcer hierarchy was a long way up the ladder from me. Jim McKay, Gifford, Jackson, Schenkel, Flemming, and Howard Cosell all had extended tenures, high national name recognition, and identity assignments that separated their status from mine. But there were others in my general arena, like Dave Diles and Bob Beattie and a woman named Andrea Kirby, who had enough on-air experience at the network to believe they were ahead of me, but who lived outside New York and couldn't hobnob with Howard, the VP of production, and Dennis Lewin, the coordinating producer for *Wide World of Sports*, as I could now.

As noted earlier, the meaningful executives were all on the 28th floor. But there were offices for staff producers and lower-level production types on the 16th, and I located an empty one that was close enough to the elevators to achieve contact with departmental traffic, and one of the green eyeshades said he knew of no reason I couldn't use it. A relatively new entry-level secretary told me she would be happy to help with ... whatever. I began going to lunch across the street at the Warwick Hotel. After a few weeks, the waiters knew my name.

The culture was like a club, and now I had membership. By the beginning of 1977, I was off the sidelines of college football for good and headed forward as a broad-based multisport play-by-play person. I could see a glimpse of the future, and it was beyond what had once been my wildest dreams.

Now there was a Roone-approved announcer the network could send to all these destinations every year, and neither the talent nor their agents had any room to squawk. So the travel schedule expanded. And now most weekends Linda was at home alone in New York while I was traveling first class, living in hotel rooms, being recognized by TV viewers in lobbies and airports, and becoming easy prey for the growing temptations of my lifestyle. I gradually learned that few of the married men I traveled with were perfectly faithful to their wives. Several of the young producers and directors were already on wife number two, most of those wives were stashed in suburban homes in Connecticut or Westchester County, and for most of the fraternity checking into a hotel was quickly followed by scouting trips to the cocktail lounge. At the office building on Sixth Avenue, most of the secretaries and other clerical staffers were young, in their 20s, and the unmistakable smell of money and power was omnipresent. I developed a wandering eye.

8

Free Agency

inda quickly found her first niche in the world of TV, working in public relations for a new concept network, a premium pay operation that had named itself Home Box Office. She was meeting interesting people and working hard while I was mostly out on the road.

It also didn't take long to forget the stern advice Keith Jackson had given me early in my first college football season, when he had sized me up enough to grudgingly acknowledge I just might have a future in the admired culture of ABC Sports. "Stay off the 28th floor," Jackson said. "Steer clear of the supercilious executives in their Paul Stuart suits and their Gucci shoes. Buy yourself a home on the sunset side of the mountains and stay as far away as you can from 1330 Sixth Avenue. Do all that and you will have a long and successful career."

The model for that was Jim McKay, who lived a train ride away in Westport, Connecticut, but almost never showed his face in the office. Nor did the overwhelming bulk of the announcer staff. The only other on-air face who regularly appeared at 1330 was Howard Cosell. On that evidence alone I should have realized how utterly warped and self-obsessed I had become.

In 1977, I began calling college football games in the play-by-play booth, trying to do so well at calling the fourth-best regional game that I could at some point elevate to the third-best regional game. I had learned about personnel management from Jackson, so I put forth a meaningful effort to evaluate candidates and recruit the best spotter and statistician I could find. Eventually, I rose high enough in the play-by-play hierarchy to call the Liberty Bowl, which ranked behind only the Sugar and Gator bowls in prestige among our network's college games. Former Olympic researcher and *Monday Night Football* statistician Terry O'Neil, who was now climbing in the ranks of producers, lobbied hard for me to get the gig, then in the aftermath told me I had been awful, talking incessantly and seeking to call attention to myself.

"Just WAY too much of you, guy!" Terry said, and when I listened back on tape I had to agree.

My mother liked it, but I knew not to put too much stock in that. As time went on, I learned that conventional sports play-by-play—football, basketball, and baseball—might not be my bread and butter.

But now I lived in New York. And like the offices, the studios were in New York. And in the ongoing style and content evolution of sports television, the studios were becoming more and more important. And in the studio, your face was always on camera. I realized my youth and vitality and quick mind might give me an edge, and I began to think more in terms of host roles.

There was a rudimentary host operation attached to *Wide World*, most used to deliver promos for future programming and break up the monotony of the event coverage. There was a bare-bones *College Football Scoreboard*, hosted by several secondary players in the division army, but it was as thin a formality as it could possibly have been, even at a time when the Sunday NFL shows were growing in prominence.

With a veteran Keith Jackson apparatchik named Jerry Klein as my lieutenant, I targeted the college football studio and worked to get Chuck Howard focused on what that could mean to us, amid rumors that CBS was going to buy into the college football rights scenario and compete with us in a sport long exclusively ruled by yellow blazers and ABC Sports patches. By 1979, I was all set up with a birdcage full of eager young information freaks, mostly college age, armed with phone lines to every college football press box in the country.

I needed a sidekick on the air. There was a former University of Pittsburgh sports information director named Carroll "Beano" Cook, a college football obsessive with a million stories, many that couldn't be told on the air, but he was witty and irreverent and an effective self-promoter. Best of all, he had gotten a lot of attention in the *Sporting News* in the fall of 1974, the first year Don Tollefson and I were on the air, with a column that decried us as the death of the sport, the worst thing television had ever done to football, and took me to task for being too handsome not to be hopelessly shallow. He had compared me to Hitler and Attila the Hun. So I told Chuck we had to get Beano to come in and sit next to me, and we did.

There was no way he would have turned down the exposure and the money.

When the production manager asked Beano what he would need to feel comfortable on the set, he asked that every Saturday he be given a dozen cans of Tab, which was the late '70s precursor to Diet Coke. A dozen, he made clear, no fewer.

By his own design, Beano came off grumpy. In the hour before we went on the air for pregame the first Saturday, one of our young, impressionable runners, Andy Baumgardner, decided to seek a conversation with him. As he dropped off some written material to him on the set, and knowing that Beano had flown in from Pittsburgh for the gig, Andy cheerfully said, "So, Mr. Cook, did you have a pleasant evening in New York last night?"

Uninterested in the kid but choosing not to blow him off, Beano looked up and asked, "What do you mean?"

"Well, did you go out to dinner or do anything social?"

"I did the same thing I always do. Checked into the room, ate a room service hamburger, masturbated, and went to sleep. Any other questions?"

And on that note Beano's tenure on the *College Football Scoreboard* began. He was a perfect sidekick for me, supportive, highly complimentary of my work, always full of utterly non-essential trivia that only the most similarly compulsive college football lovers would know. He drank a dozen full cans of Tab on the set every Saturday, and we worked together for several years. I never asked if in this role he saw me as Hitler or Attila the Hun. That was ancient history, which only helped me to realize that when someone in parallel media attacks you in public, he or she only makes you bigger. I was one of the biggest media voices in college football at that time, and Beano Cook was helpful in making me that way.

———

By the first half of 1978, a year and a half after Linda and I had moved from Chapel Hill to New York, my travel schedule had exploded.

Central to that was the *Wide World* syndrome, within which I was off week after week to remote locations for the exotic events that had over the years become on-air institutions. Those excursions were in addition to regional football games in the fall now that I had graduated from the sidelines to play-by-play. But I was still doing videotaped features and interviews for air on the A-game football telecast, so it wasn't unusual for me to arrive back in New York on Sunday (or if I was lucky, late Saturday night), and then be off on another plane Tuesday morning for college football or *Wide World*. Or both.

I was a low-cost, high-intensity asset for the network, and for both sides it made good sense to exploit that. Linda was the most loyal and devoted wife I could ever have imagined, so if there was a threat to my marriage at that point, it would emerge from my too-frequent flirtations away from home.

But at the same time Linda and I had migrated north in 1976, my closest male friend from Chapel Hill had finished law school and was stepping into an entry-level deal with a Manhattan law firm. And for the next year and a half our lives were liberally intermingled as Linda helped him set up and furnish his West Side apartment, helped him select dating prospects to fill his social calendar, went in companionship with him to UNC-based social events that were frequent and made sense for them when I was out of town. I never gave a moment's thought to the notion that might be the source of a coming breakup.

I was the one who was going to bars hundreds of miles away from New York and entertaining the advances of women who knew my face from TV. Linda's willpower was bound to be sturdier than mine. I was sure of that.

So it came as a surprise when I returned from motorcycle speed week in Daytona Beach in 1978 and Linda casually asked, "Do you have any idea how many nights you have been home in the past month?"

Shocked, I fished for the logical number in my mind. "I don't know. Maybe five?"

"It's three."

"Okay, makes sense. But who's counting?"

"I'm counting, and that shouldn't really surprise you, should it?"

"Maybe not, but why are you counting?"

The answer was my best friend's name, Stan Davis. I learned that night they were pretty far along. We stayed up collaborating on a farewell audio tape containing every Jackson Browne ballad that had ever brought us to tears. The following day Linda took the bulk of her stuff and moved to his place on the West Side. I deeply loved them both, and I was sincerely happy for them. I was happy for all of us that there were no children involved. I was happy for me that I would no longer feel guilty about my misbehavior on the road.

I am still best friends with Linda, who is now another marriage beyond the one she shared for decades with my buddy the lawyer, and we compare our lives via text.

Many times, I have tried to take the blame for the dissolution of that marriage, but Linda firmly rejects that assertion. She has led a happy life despite various real-world challenges, and her friendship is a priceless treasure, just as it was when she was the only really cool person at Southwest Miami High School who would give me the time of day.

I went forward on a path of working life success and personal life chaos. Few who have as much wreckage on their resumes as I do can live without any regret, and I have plenty.

I was nowhere near displacing Keith Jackson on college football, and Keith was still young enough for me to expect to never get there. That was fine once the studio scoreboard operation became a strong presence. When Al Michaels came over from CBS to do the A-game on the baseball telecasts, I knew for sure the backup/rain-delay game would be the height of my ambitions there, and that was fine, too. I did not have the refined baseball knowledge and instincts to function as the central play-by-play figure there. But basketball? I mean . . . I had done the DEAN SMITH show. How could I fall short there?

Reality in the middle '70s was no basketball presence at ABC Sports.

Years before, and for a significant period of time, the network had covered the NBA, and there was a famous in-house story of how Roone Arledge's partiality to star power had prompted him to hire Bob Cousy as an expert commentator without acknowledging and accounting for Cousy's speech affectations that caused him to mispronounce words, one of which was in this instance the boss's name. That emerged when Arledge first met Cousy at courtside before a game, and the NBA all-time great stuck out his hand and said, "Hi Woone, Bob Cousy." Shortly, other arrangements were made.

And by the time I arrived, the NBA package had moved to another network, leaving former Columbia University All-America distance-shooting legend Chet Forte to focus on sports other than his own, including *Monday Night Football*.

But then a one-off happened, giving me the chance to appear on a basketball telecast. Somehow the network acquired the rights to the championship game of the 1978 Atlantic Coast Conference tournament. Since Chuck Howard (Duke) and I (UNC) were habitually talking basketball and jousting with each other over ACC results, it only made sense that he assigned me to the game that became the *Wide World of Sports* feature on Saturday afternoon, March 4, from the Greensboro Coliseum.

It was a national telecast, and I wasn't yet to be trusted with that kind of play-by-play assignment, so the role was as a sideline/bench reporter in my yellow ABC blazer. There was an ancillary thrill, because in casting about for an expert commentator, the network had made a deal with the great Bill Russell, and as a lifetime Celtics fan who worshipped his championship record and his outspoken commitment to civil rights, I admired him and couldn't have described in words my excitement when Forte invited me to his room the night before the semifinal games—Wake Forest vs. UNC, Duke vs. Maryland—to meet Russell.

I went in while Russell and Chet were playing gin rummy with a couple of other people. The great No. 6 barely noticed me, but at some point it was mentioned to him that I was a Carolina alum and knew Dean Smith. For a few seconds, I felt great pride. Then Russell looked right at me.

"Well, I hope you're going to be okay with losing tomorrow. Dean Smith is an awful coach. That four corners offense thing is an atrocity.

He's wasted more good talent than any other coach I know. And tomorrow night he's going to lose to Wake Forest. So don't be all brokenhearted when it happens."

Laughter filled the room. I didn't know for sure whether it was all a big joke or whether Russell meant every word he said, but it was clearly no time and place for me to push that issue. Heartbroken—Coach Smith was at that time my No. 1 most irreproachable idol—I hung around long enough to finish one beer and then slink off back to my room.

The following night, as Russell had predicted, Wake Forest upset the Tar Heels in what would be the great Phil Ford's last ACC game in a Carolina uniform, and I was in a double gloomy funk. Russell was entitled to his opinion, and sometimes your most revered idols can be dead wrong about something. Unless he was doing it at Chet's behest just to pull my leg, which might or might not have been even worse.

To make matters more cruel, the championship game we were calling turned out to be between Wake Forest and Duke, the Tar Heels' bitter basketball rival. The Blue Devils not only won their first ACC title in 12 years, but they also went on to reach the Final Four in St. Louis and defeat Notre Dame and Digger Phelps in the semifinals before losing to Kentucky on Monday night due mostly to a 41-point performance by Jack "Goose" Givens.

By the time ABC acquired an ongoing involvement in college basketball, it was 1987, Roone had been displaced as the division chieftain, and his successor was in the process of forcing me and Chuck Howard out of our jobs. Later, I called one college basketball game on CBS and one NBA game (Spurs vs. Clippers) on NBC. In both instances the boss was looking for me to succeed, which probably would have led to a regular assignment, and I got no real feedback after the telecast and was never assigned to courtside again. So Dean Smith or no Dean Smith, I can only surmise that I wasn't any good at calling basketball.

You can't always get what you want, period.

9

Reggie and "Stacks"

When Linda abruptly moved across Central Park to her new West Side life with my best friend, I collected unanticipated benefits. Our rent-controlled two-bedroom apartment was converted to a co-op, and I became sole owner of a property worth far more than I paid for it. Soon I would sublet it to the statistician who worked on my college football play-by-play assignments, adding to my income as I relocated to a more glamorous high-rise several blocks farther south on Madison Avenue.

Meanwhile I was gradually making the transition from my initial ABC Sports status as a gimmick innovation to a legitimized member of the most high-profile announcer staff in television sports. I had been replaced on the college football sideline, first in 1977 by a woman named Anne Simon, then the following season by a former Maryland Terrapins player named Tim Brant. On regional football weekends I did play-by-play on the third-largest or fourth-largest regional game. When there was only one nationally televised game, I was often assigned to *Wide World of Sports*.

I was still gathering steam in college-town bars, and in New York I was increasingly omnipresent in the saloons along Third Avenue, where stories were propagated for the popular social record of that moment, a *New York Post* subsection titled "Page Six." I was fascinated to note that the one person most adept at creating personal buzz through that vehicle was not an athlete or a showbiz personality, but of all things a real estate developer. I didn't even know what that entailed. His name was Donald Trump. I was first introduced to him at P.J. Clarke's restaurant and bar. Then later at Jim McMullen's. Then again at Elaine's. I began to gather that real estate development was perceived as a gateway to money. It wasn't at first clear how much.

But money was endemic to the biggest change in the culture of American sports circa the late 1970s; the sudden arrival of free agency. A small handful of baseball players were successfully challenging the so-called reserve clause—the clause in their major league contracts that restricted them from negotiating with another team upon the expiration of the deal—and exploiting the marketplace at levels of compensation never seen in American sports. For New Yorkers, that meant 1977 was the first year Reggie Jackson spent in Yankees pinstripes.

I had first met Reggie in the off season, when in early January I had been sent to the most coveted of all *Wide World* assignments: three surfing competitions on the North Shore of Oahu: the Duke Kahanamoku Surfing Classic, the Pipeline Masters, and the Masters Female Surf. The work could extend to a couple of weeks if the weather was slow to cooperate with high breakers. That meant long days on the beach at the Kahala Hilton Hotel and long nights at a Waikiki bar/restaurant called Rex and Eric's, where Reggie was a regular in the backgammon lounge and the discotheque.

And if you spent even 10 minutes in that disco, you were sure to be friendly with the deejay, a dramatic brunette with a loud laugh named

Joanne Faith Mallis. To say she was outgoing was a vast understatement. She controlled a packed and deafening room every night, spinning and dancing, dancing and spinning, hugging every regular customer as they gradually filed in from dinner and drinks.

I met Reggie in the bar, and along with surfing director Andy Sidaris was introduced to Joanne in the disco. Andy didn't really know her name, so he theatrically presented her to me as "stacks of wax," referencing the pile of 45 rpm discs stacked up next to her turntables. (And in that moment Andy coined for her a nickname that stuck for the rest of her life, though when Ethel Kennedy and her children later shortened it to "Stacks," it became more difficult to explain. Joanne didn't seem to notice. She simply liked that General Maxwell Taylor called her "Stacks" at Ethel Kennedy's lunch table just past the maître d' stand at the 21 club in New York.)

Reggie made clear to me he saw himself as Joanne's protector at Rex and Eric's. I couldn't tell what that entailed, other than that they knew each other and laughed uproariously at each other's jokes. But everything within reach of her was an uproar. She had explosive energy and a dance playlist that lingered in my mind for weeks. Or months.

Until I saw Joanne next about six months later on a Manhattan street corner, waiting for a bus at Fifth Avenue and 53rd Street. I wasn't sure she remembered me, but the fact she was waiting for a bus instead of hailing a cab or boarding a limo gave me functional control. I was single, we began dating, and I appreciated her telling me from the start she was seeing Reggie, too. They were "just friends." He was "like a big brother" to her.

I believed it because I wanted to, and we were off and running. I had seen photos of Reggie with another woman, identified as a girlfriend, on Page Six. Sometimes we would meet up after a game on the East Side and all dine together.

New York was lonely without a main squeeze, and now I had one. Her elder sister was a famous architect. Her middle sister was a high-powered

PR rep in fashion and design. Now I could go to Studio 54 with no worry about being recognized at the door. If I wanted, I could sit at Andy Warhol's table.

As it is with many adolescents, college didn't turn out as planned. That was Joanne, who grew up in an East Brooklyn waterside neighborhood. Pressured by a James Madison High School guidance counselor to apply *somewhere*, she had chosen New Mexico State for the modern architecture she saw in the brochure. It wasn't until she landed in Las Cruces that she discovered an agricultural and mining school. The bounce had sent her all the way to Rex and Eric's on Kalākaua Avenue, where she was a Honolulu-sized star.

Now she was back in New York and spending most of her time at my apartment. My friends from North Carolina met Joanne and their first impressions were that it was a bad match. We ran into Linda Lee Lampley (now Davis) at a thrift store one weekend, and she was wearing a *Have you lost your mind?* expression. That made it imperative to go forward.

When Reggie hit three home runs that fall against the Dodgers in Game 6 of the World Series, Joanne and I were there on tickets comped by Mister October himself.

When word got around at 1330 Sixth Avenue that I was social with him, I became the designated network-level Yankees locker-room guy. And when I really needed a tough access, a harder-to-get interview, number 44 would set it up for me.

If you liked anyone at all in that locker room, you liked 44. He was genuinely a prince, along with pitching star Ron Guidry, the nicest and most cooperative personality in an otherwise inflexible group. And they were not the only major superstars I knew to behave that way.

Ten years later in Los Angeles I found that Earvin "Magic" Johnson carried exactly that same trait. After tough losses, he greeted reporters at the Lakers' locker room door with a welcoming smile. If you didn't like

Magic Johnson, you probably didn't really like anyone. Even Larry Bird liked Magic Johnson.

———————

Joanne Mallis and I were opposites who attracted at first. She was disco personified. I was strictly rock and roll. She was Brooklyn; I was Hendersonville and Chapel Hill. I had an undergraduate degree in English and a graduate school transcript that could become a master's degree if I ever sat still for a couple of months and wrote a thesis. She had the weekend at New Mexico State that didn't turn out like she'd planned.

I had a well-connected squadron of age-20-something friends at ABC Sports who worked and played together. Terry O'Neil (Notre Dame '73) was a fast-rising producer who had first gained notoriety as the Olympic researcher who somehow had a bio on Soviet gymnast Olga Korbut at Munich in 1972 (even the Russian Federation knew next to nothing about her). Terry had also been Frank Gifford's statistician on *Monday Night Football*. Dorrance Smith (Claremont '73) had become my college football feature producer early in my first season on the sidelines. Ric LaCivita (Harvard '74) succeeded Dorrance a year later as my closest friend and traveling companion. Jeff Ruhe (Stanford '74) had vaulted from production assistant to becoming Roone Arledge's personal associate when Dick Ebersol abruptly left ABC to go down the street to NBC. Jeff was also dating Robert F. Kennedy's middle daughter, Courtney, which earned all of us eligibility for touch football games at Hickory Hill. Sean McManus (Duke '75) was a production assistant and Jim McKay's son and later the longtime head of CBS Sports.

I was at first apprehensive about blending Joanne into what I saw through my insecure filters as a socially rarified group. I couldn't have been more wrong. They all wanted to dance at Studio 54, and she had the connections to get us in. And she shared with Courtney and her mother, Ethel, an abiding love for cigarettes, white wine, and french fries with mayonnaise. The Kennedys barely bothered to notice my devoted liberal politics, but they all noticed the dark drama of Joanne Mallis. It wasn't terribly long before "she's with Jim Lampley" gave way to "he's with Stacks." Courtney and Ethel couldn't get enough of her.

So when it became clear that Courtney Kennedy was going to become Mrs. Jeff Ruhe, and in light of the inescapable reality I had already once been married and divorced, a certain pressure began to ratchet up. If there had been any competition at all between Reggie Jackson and me—and looking back, I'm pretty certain that was a delusion—it surely didn't exist now. When I was on the road, I was on the phone with Joanne. When I was in New York, I was working or with Joanne.

When my mother came to the city to visit me, she was at first taken back by Joanne's brassiness. But Mom was quickly charmed by her parents, who were earthy in a big way, and her sisters, who were educated and sophisticated.

Me? I had seldom felt more weak willed and out of control. Joanne had a disco music promotion job at a big label, Arista Records, which required her several times a week to go out to dance clubs in sexy dresses until all hours. I had given her a credit card, and when she walked back and forth to the office on 57th Street, it would cost me hundreds of dollars a day.

I don't know how or where we got ahold of a marriage license. It was April 1979, and I was in London for the Rugby League Challenge Cup final with a crowd of 94,000 rowdy fans, most of them Yorkshiremen who had prepped overnight with countless ales on the train ride from the North country. The expert commentator was American football star Cris Collinsworth, working behind a microphone for the first time. We had a blast, and I don't believe I told him I might again be getting married upon arrival back in New York the following day.

The limo showed up at JFK carrying Joanne, her sister Fern the famous PR rep, and a strikingly handsome architect friend named Scott Bromley. They were drinking champagne. We all donned matching cranberry polo shirts and went straight to a justice of the peace in the Bronx. Now I was married again on the very day I turned 30.

That night I was whisked to a surprise birthday party thrown by dozens of my close friends from Chapel Hill. The venue was the Broome Street Bar in Soho, coincidentally the first place I had taken Joanne on a date a little less than two years before. The idea was for all my closest friends to surprise me on my 30th. By the end of the evening, they were the ones most surprised. It would be more accurate to say "shocked." They had never even met Joanne.

When I called my mother to give her the news, she didn't try to muster enthusiasm. "Well, I just hope you will take this marriage more seriously than you did the first one."

I couldn't have said it better myself.

10

My Miracle on Ice

"I Still Believe in Miracles" (PCN Photography/Alamy Stock Photo)

The greatest and most inspiring of all American sports stories took place in a setting that was almost comical in its inadequacy.

The 1980 Winter Olympics had been awarded to the tiny

village of Lake Placid, New York, because after a 48-year absence, it was time for the Winter Games to return to America. The 1932 event had been situated there in the Adirondacks, and most critically, among all the winter resorts in the United States to that moment, only a couple of them had a world-class bobsled and luge track. Squaw Valley was the site of the Winter Games in 1960, so it was Lake Placid's turn, and there wasn't much more to it than that.

But the Olympics had changed dramatically since 1932. Television had vastly expanded the audience, and the increasingly dramatic interplay of flags and anthems at their core had amplified their sociopolitical impact. So the TV promotional phrase ABC used to prepare viewers for immersion, "The world comes to Lake Placid," was but a thin veil over the immense challenge the residents and organizers there were facing.

There weren't enough hotel rooms. There weren't enough buses and trains. There weren't enough restaurants and convenience stores. There weren't enough portable toilets. There wasn't enough anything, and many observers with deep Olympics experience, especially producers and executives at ABC Sports, could see problems arising. The city manager from New Orleans, whom the local organizers had brought in to troubleshoot, held daily fantasy-based news briefings at which a story of complex preparedness was fronted, and penetrating questions were ignored.

As I wrote on a UNC website in April 2020, a bigger story was brewing, a front-page blockbuster involving Soviet tanks on the streets of Kabul, Afghanistan. The Jimmy Carter administration was urged to push back against that, and the degree to which the 1980 Summer Games, scheduled for later that year in Moscow, might become a bargaining chip in that confrontation.

This came at a time when 52 Americans were being held hostage by Iranian students at the American embassy in Tehran, and a complicated patchwork of global oil politics had conspired to create desperate shortages of gasoline and oil in the United States in recent months. A presidential election loomed in November. Carter needed a win. Some kind of a win.

The hostage crisis was humiliating, the Soviet tanks in Afghanistan were humiliating, and for average Americans nothing was more humiliating than rising in darkness at 3:30 or 4 AM for an interminable wait somewhere to buy a tank of gas. So it wasn't just the president who was desperate. The whole country was looking for a proverbial shot in the arm, similar to what happened in the COVID pandemic.

Lake Placid was my third Olympics with ABC Sports. Right up until two weeks before the opening ceremony, my assignment was to handle play-by-play for the bobsled and luge competitions. But as the picture came into focus, it became clear these games would be a political event. Significant stories emerged on two fronts: On the local level, there was the obvious inability of local organizers to accommodate large numbers of people coming from all over the globe into a tiny town with little infrastructure, as well as a complex makeshift transportation scenario that was untested and highly questionable on its face. That was the micro front, and alongside it emerged the macro: the sudden desire of the Carter administration to move, delay, or cancel the Moscow Summer Games scheduled for five months later, as a political protest of the Soviet troops in Afghanistan.

With only a few days to go, my Lake Placid assignment was switched, and now I would be the designated political reporter covering those stories for ABC Sports and ABC News.

As the games got underway, I was busy: sometimes racing out to the local airport to interview Assistant Secretary of State Hodding Carter or Secretary of State Cyrus Vance as they landed to negotiate with the International Olympic Committee; sometimes covering news conferences at which local organizing committee executive Petr Spurney spewed falsehoods about his busing system or ticket distribution. Meanwhile, reports rolled in about thousands of ticket holders freezing in remote parking lots waiting for buses that never arrived.

In the games themselves, there was one early medal hope dashed: a groin injury during a warm-up debilitated pairs figure skater Randy Gardner, reducing him and his skilled and glamorous partner Tai Babilonia to spectator status. America's most heavily favored competitor, speed skater Eric Heiden, began grinding out his dominant gold performances, setting four Olympic records en route to fulfilling his destiny as the greatest champion ever in his sport. But speed skating was too esoteric for most American TV viewers to bond with emotionally. What made it interesting: the night before the opening ceremony, a lightly regarded American hockey team got a slap-shot goal in the final 30 seconds to tie heavily favored Sweden.

The gold medalist in hockey was a foregone conclusion. The Soviet national team was the most impregnable juggernaut in international team sports, gold medalist in five of the last six Olympics and 14 of the last 17 World Championships. The previous year the Soviets had won two of three games against a team of NHL All-Stars in the Challenge Cup.

The American team couldn't have been more opposite, a hand-to-mouth aggregate of college players and minor leaguers with no perceived chance at competing for a medal. A few days before the opening ceremony, the Americans finished up a 61-game pre-Olympic prep schedule with a marquee matchup against the Soviets at Madison Square Garden. The final score was 10–3, and in retrospect it seemed clear the Russians had gone easy on their outmanned opponent. Many media types observed it could easily have been 20–3.

So there was no overwhelming public notice on the first night of competition when the Americans got what amounted to an upset draw with Sweden on Bill Baker's blue line slap shot. Nor were there blaring headlines two nights later when they stunned powerful Czechoslovakia with a seven-goal outburst. Then there were wins over Norway, Romania, and West Germany, and surprisingly, in week two of the Olympics, the Americans were headed toward the four-team medal round. But cold reality stared them in the face: a semifinal matchup with Russia's big red machine, scheduled for 5 PM Friday afternoon.

Now that the American team had become a story in an Olympics largely devoid of noteworthy American headlines, ABC and Team USA approached the event authorities about moving the game to prime time. But the Soviets refused, and ABC was reduced to telegraphing to the audience that USA vs. Russia hockey would be tape-recorded and broadcast in prime time, in effect a three-hour delay.

It was February 22, 1980. At five o'clock I was seated in a videotape edit bay in the ABC broadcast center, supervising the composition of a compendium feature that would tie together my two weeks of stories, scheduled for airing on the Sunday afternoon closing ceremony show.

As my producer and an editor worked through the material, we all glanced from time to time at a tiny monitor mounted above the side of the edit bay, a four-by-six-inch screen on which the hockey game was airing live. A frenetic first period was winding down, and in the closing seconds we were watching out of the corners of our eyes as American star Mark Johnson chased a loose puck inside the Soviet blue line just in time to wrist-roll it into a corner of the net. Officials had to check a replay to be certain Johnson's last stab had beaten the clock. It had. Amazingly, the game was tied 2–2 with two periods to go.

At that time, every ABC Sports facility, whether an office or a control room or a technical facility, was equipped with a red telephone. Years before I had been instructed to understand the red phone was called the "Roone phone," and if it ever rang, the voice at the other end would be the legendary chief executive of the sports division, the executive producer of every sports program the network produced, Roone Arledge. Ten seconds after Mark Johnson's goal, the red phone rang, an event I had never witnessed in six years at ABC. A quick assessment of the personnel in the edit bay established that I was the senior participant, so I picked up the receiver and instantly recognized Roone's voice.

"Is Jim Lampley there?"

"Yes, Roone, it's me."

"What are you doing?" I ran it down for him.

"Drop that right now. If something unusual happens in the hockey game, we are going to need an interview to button it up before we go off the air. Get over to that arena and make sure you can give us what we need. You just became our most important asset tonight."

Arledge was legendary in television for his golden gut, the inexplicable ability to sense that something dramatic was about to happen before it happened. As events played out, never had that gut been more golden. Before I hung up the phone, I pointed out one possible obstacle.

"Roone, I don't have the right credential to get into hockey."

"You'll get in." He hung up.

Getting into Olympic events without the right credential was well known to be borderline impossible, just two Olympics removed from the Munich kidnapping of Israeli athletes. But now I had no choice. My colleagues were smiling at my predicament as I bolted out the door.

Some things happen just because they are supposed to. When I reached the Lake Placid High School hockey rink, the person who greeted me at the door was the venue manager, whom I happened randomly to have met just a few days before. He let me in. The next challenge was to find a logical place to watch where I wouldn't be removed by ushers. I climbed onto a camera platform about 40 feet behind the announcer table where Al Michaels and Ken Dryden were calling the game.

As the second period progressed, I struggled to stand still so as not to interfere with the work of two operators who were manning the primary game coverage cameras. There was another man on the platform who also didn't belong there, and I recognized him: a famous Long Island folk-rocker named Harry Chapin, who had performed in a concert in the Olympic Village the night before. While I was a fan, it was no time for greetings. But Chapin was distracting enough that I failed to notice at first a striking event that had taken place in the Soviet net. Apparently infuriated by the Johnson goal, Russian coach Viktor Tikhonov had yanked the undisputed world's greatest goalie, Vladislav Tretiak, and replaced him with lesser regarded backup Anatoly Myshkin.

That didn't matter at first as the drama ratcheted up. The Soviets were controlling play in the second period, but they struggled to score. As the period ended, they led 3–2, so numerically the scrappy Americans still had a chance. There were 20 minutes to go. Chapin and I still hadn't shared a word, and he disappeared into a restroom. I spent the intermission chatting with the cameramen and doubling down on a promise to stay still and protect their camera shots.

As the third period began, the Russians resumed their tactical command on the ice, but American goalie Jim Craig, a college player from the Boston area, was now a different person than at any previous time in his life. In hockey it is called "standing on your head"—that experience when suddenly no shot is good enough to pierce a goalie's wall, no matter who is firing the puck and from where. The high school arena crowd began to sound like a full stadium. The faces of the Russian veterans began to clench up in frustration. With just under 12 minutes to go, diminutive Mark Johnson, who for two weeks had suddenly been the hottest goal scorer in the world, slipped the puck under Myshkin's mitt and it was tied, 3–3.

That arena was huge for high school hockey. It seated 8,500 people, and the spontaneous roar that greeted Johnson's second goal of the game made them sound like 85,000. Harry Chapin and I hadn't yet exchanged a word, but simultaneously we leaped into each other's arms and began jumping up and down, prompting both camera operators to turn and shout at us to calm down. From the beginning there had been a smattering of American flags visible in the crowd, but suddenly it was as though someone had passed out another 6,000 of them. That crowd was now a rocking ocean of red, white, and blue. And as play began again, the Soviet players looked mystified, as though they had been dropped off in a world they had never seen.

If you know anything at all about this story, you know that fewer than two minutes later a minor league journeyman named Mike Eruzione scored the most famous single goal in the history of hockey. You know that in the closing four minutes, Jim Craig stood on his head like no other goalie at any level ever has, and you know that despite a relentless escalating assault from the greatest hockey team in the world, the Americans held on for the 4–3 win. You can imagine that Harry Chapin and I shared one more bouncing celebratory hug, then we bolted off the camera platform and never said a word to each other. Not one. And you realize that I was there with an assignment, and my work was just beginning.

I raced downstairs to the hallway outside the American locker room, where player after player stepped wet from the shower out the door into the media crush and amid the noise and chaos turned away from my frenzied shouting and disappeared into the opposite hallway. The last face to appear was that of Mike Eruzione. We had the same agent, and he was the only player on the team I had actually met. He knew my voice.

To this day millions of Americans believe, or want to believe, that they watched a live telecast of the game, climaxing with Al Michaels's legendary play-by-play call as the clock dwindled: "Do you BELIEVE in miracles?" It's somehow too incongruous for the majority of viewers to place in their mind's eyes and ears that the game began at 5 PM, most of the true hockey fans in the audience were still at work, and millions more fans watched it on videotape and thought they had seen it live.

While most of America watched the game that night, I stashed Eruzione, Craig, and Craig's dad at one of the few real restaurants in Lake Placid. Their dinner was a blur. It was nearly impossible to have a conversation as the tiny Italian restaurant adjusted to the realization of who was sitting there at our table.

It became a near-deafening pep rally, with seemingly everyone in the room continuously shouting the new theme of those Olympics: "USA! USA! USA!"

At 10:45 I led Mike and Jimmy to a spot in the middle of the main drag to face a camera, and as we waited for host Jim McKay to toss it to me for the interview, a large crowd assembled behind and around us. Eruzione, who was clever, leaned over and whispered, "Lamps, if we had come out and stood here at this point last night?" I got it. "No one would have noticed."

In the 40 years since that night, I have run into Jim Craig and Mike Eruzione a handful of times at Olympics-related events. Whenever it happens, I find a moment to lean into Mike and whisper to him, "Mike, through the miracle of videotape you are now the leading goal scorer in the history of hockey," and every time, properly cued, he answers, "Lamps, it keeps going in, doesn't it?" And it does. And it is still a miracle.

Two days later, before noon on a Sunday morning, a frenzied three-goal third-period rally brought them from behind to beat Finland for the gold medal. Another incongruity almost impossible to believe in retrospect: had they lost to Finland there would have been no medal at all, not even bronze.

And in the locker room afterward, I had the duty of taking a hard line phone call from the White House and with Vice President Walter

Mondale passing the receiver around to coach Herb Brooks and the players so President Carter could distribute congratulations to the newly minted and never to be forgotten American heroes. It wasn't Carter's win, but he would have been crazy not to take the opportunity to share in it.

And at this moment, it's encouraging to note: It didn't end the Cold War. It didn't free the hostages in Tehran. It didn't lower the price of gas. The United States DID go forward with the boycott of Moscow, and hundreds of Summer Olympics athletes lost their precious chance to compete before the eyes of the world. But the "Miracle on Ice" did provide one of countless examples of how the affairs of the playing field can heighten and enlighten the state of the world with the definitive rationality of the scoreboard, borne aloft by the irrationality of hope.

"Never say die" was conceived as a metaphor, but sometimes impossible dreams do in fact come true.

———

Storytelling is about editing. What to leave in, what to leave out. Some of this you may know, some you probably don't. So in the interest of maximum information, here are the footnotes:

It was probably because a loss to that American team was inconceivable that Soviet coach Viktor Tikhonov, infuriated by Johnson's goal that tied it at 2-2 at the first-period buzzer, yanked the greatest goalie alive, Vladislav Tretiak, and replaced him with less capable backup Vladimir Myshkin. In the wake of the loss, the reaction of the Soviet power structure focused on the impact of that impulse: Tikhonov disappeared. Eruzione and Craig told me at dinner they and their teammates were shocked and encouraged to see Myshkin between the posts as period two began. They had every reason to believe they could never beat Tretiak, but Myshkin was a different story.

From the category of "statistics are for losers," the Soviets amassed 39 shots on goal, 18 of them in the third period hailstorm Craig stared down. The United States got its four goals on a total of 16 shots.

After months of having purposely alienated every player on the team with vicious tirades and relentless criticism, all part of a preconceived strategy to get them to go onto the ice and play against *him* instead of the opposition, coach Herb Brooks saw his dream reach fruition in the stupefying takedown of the Soviets. He stood at the edge of the ice and watched the most ecstatic celebration in American sports history unfold. He even momentarily put his right foot onto the ice, a sure sign he wanted to join them. Then he pivoted and escaped through the tunnel behind the bench. Unfinished business. There was one more game to play.

When less than 44 hours later the team skated lethargically through the first two periods of the gold medal game vs. Finland and trailed 2–1 going to the third, the players sat terrified in their tiny locker room waiting for Brooks to enter, bracing for the most fire-breathing tirade of all.

Eruzione told me later he was literally trembling, and he was the oldest, most experienced player in the room. With nine minutes of the ten-minute intermission having gone by, assistant coach Craig Patrick stuck his head into the room and said, "Lace 'em up." They looked at each other in astonishment. Thirty seconds later the heavy metal door swung open and slammed noisily against the wall. With the door framing his rigid body and his face flaming red, Brooks shouted, "If you lose this game, you will take it to your graves!!! TO YOUR FUCKING GRAVES!!!" And the door slammed again. Greatest locker room pep talk in the history of sports.

Just as there is a great hockey phrase for what Jimmy Craig did on Friday night, there is also a classic description for what happened next. "Feeding frenzy." Two goals in fewer than five minutes and a third later on, and the job was done.

Seventeen months later, Harry Chapin died in a fiery car-truck collision en route to a concert on the Long Island Expressway. I never formally met him.

One year after the miracle I traveled with Herb Brooks to do a retrospective feature piece for ABC at the Lake Placid High arena. Coming back to New York in a small chartered plane, we got caught up in a wildly violent thunderstorm, with winds so overwhelming it seemed impossible for the pilot to keep control. We even laughed together at the thought that if it happened, he would get the headline and I would be a secondary footnote. We were diverted from the intended landing in Westchester and sent to Teterboro Airport in New Jersey. The following morning on the front page of the *New York Times* was a story that seven business execs had died in a small plane crash at Westchester within a few minutes of our plea to controllers to let us land there. The number was revised to eight dead—six execs, two pilots—the day after that.

Twenty-two years later, Herb Brooks was returning from a fundraiser in northeastern Minnesota when his car ran off an interstate highway and rolled over. He died without wearing his seat belt.

I'm still here. And yes, I DO believe in miracles.

11

1980s Endurance Races

t was only one seven- or eight-minute interview in a two-and-a-half week reporting effort, but the Miracle on Ice interview with Mike Eruzione and Jim Craig changed my status at ABC Sports. As soon as the games were over and we were back into a normal post-Olympic programming period, I could feel the difference.

Roone Arledge was in the middle of a sustained drive toward building a memorable legacy as a sports and news producer and chief executive. At Lake Placid, I was functional in both areas. I could be trusted to handle any *Wide World* segment, from the cultural extremities of the New York State firemen's competition to the bread and butter of the USA Track and Field Championships. I was an event-coverage workhorse, as a studio host, as a serious sports journalist, as a reporter who could perform under the news banner or the sports banner. I had been at three Olympics already.

During my first five years at the network level, the NFL studio shows had evolved into juggernaut star-making machinery for NBC and CBS. I was busy urging ABC Sports executives to do the same with our college football studio. And I sensed, as we got back to New York from Lake Placid, that Arledge had a new reason to care what I thought.

With Arledge in charge of both ABC divisions, I had begun to collect occasional assignments covering sports subjects for news programming, and my identity broadened. All that went to another level at Lake Placid in 1980, where international politics interacted with the most glamorous of sports events to demonstrate their increasing influence on each other. And my connections with the hockey team had drawn the attention of an ambitious new TV sports agent.

Arthur C. Kaminsky was a New-York-born-and-bred hockey fanatic with diplomas from Cornell (undergraduate) and Yale (law school). While the smooth and urbane Barry Frank had been gathering a clientele focused on recognizable network TV sports figures, Art Kaminsky was assembling his own roster dominated by National Hockey League players, along with a sprinkling of media types. Art represented Herb Brooks, the coach who was now a red-white-and-blue hero for having guided the hockey miracle. He represented John Powers, the *Boston Globe* writer with whom he was now completing a book journaling that adventure. He repped Terry O'Neil, the hottest and most fiercely independent young ABC Sports producer. And now I learned from Terry that Kaminsky wanted to take me to lunch at the legendary Friars Club.

The Friars Club was a hangout for comedians and Broadway actors and literary types. It wasn't the kind of place where I might bump into Barry Frank, who was far more likely to be at 21 or the Four Seasons. That cultural difference was part of Art's pitch, and he was in no way bashful about it. I had graduated to the place where the network now needed me at least as much as I needed them. If I were on the market, CBS and NBC likely would make substantial offers, but all the top ABC executives were Barry's friends and golf partners. So did I want to capitalize on my growing identity—or not?

I lay awake for a few nights contemplating all this, and eventually I bit. I had no signed paper with Barry Frank; it was just a matter of making the phone call and enduring the 15-minute treatise on why this was a big mistake. Once that was done, I went to Kaminsky's cramped Manhattan office, overflowing with newspapers he had collected for their significance and impact (like August 8, 1974, the day Nixon resigned), and we devised a strategy for changing my world.

The last thing I asked him was: "Is there a chance I am going to wind up on the street?" He was scathingly dismissive. "Are you kidding? You're going to wind up in the penthouse!" It was his metaphorical way of saying we were playing with house money.

With Art's guidance I began to pursue a more aggressive campaign in the sports division, gradually relinquishing the feeling that I was lucky in my unprecedented position in favor of believing that they were fortunate to have my diversified talent. There was no one in my generation making regular appearances as a play-by-play voice or a host on CBS as the 1980s began. That didn't happen until I had solidified my hold on the ABC college football studio, and in 1985 CBS Sports chief Neal Pilson brought in Jim Nantz from a station in Houston to go head-to-head with me. It was fun to watch him work back then because he was 10 years my junior, and it was clear he could have an eye-catching career.

It was also fun because before Pilson recruited Nantz, he had pursued serious discussions with Art about whether I would leave ABC and jump to CBS, and those discussions had become the fulcrum for a new contract at higher compensation, with more elevated *Wide World* exposures at remotes and in the studio.

Farther down Sixth Avenue at NBC, Bob Costas had built exposure as a baseball play-by-play prodigy and NFL studio host, even while still holding down a hockey play-by-play job in St. Louis. It was easy to notice his powerful on-air presence and comfort, and that he was headed toward an epic career if he kept his life in order. As it turned out, Nantz and Costas did a better job of keeping their personal lives in order than I did, but in the early 1980s that wasn't a defining issue.

Looking through the filter of a three-network world, I had the best position. ABC had a near-exclusive hold on the Olympics, which was notable. ABC also had *Monday Night Football,* and Art was moving me toward meaningful involvement there. ABC owned ESPN, a rapidly rising force that would broaden television involvement across all corners of the sports landscape. And Jim McKay and Howard Cosell were seemingly on the verge of aging out. Armed with my new contract and newly empowered by my aggressive, insurgent agent, I was thinking of how to maximize my involvement in *Wide World* and the Olympics.

———

Wide World of Sports did have a studio element, but it wasn't a force in the weekly flow of topical sports information, except for when Howard Cosell arranged for Muhammad Ali to come in and create a news event.

I thought of pushing the power structure to alter that, but I knew from a couple of unpleasant meetings with Jim McKay at the 1976 Winter and Summer Olympics that he wouldn't support it. Whether that was because McKay really felt sports fans were uncomfortable with shows on serious issues, or because coverage of that type might elevate my profile as a reporter, I couldn't tell for sure. I had been a bit surprised in the first few years at how friendly and warm older hands like Chris Schenkel, Frank Gifford, and Bill Flemming had been to me.

Keith Jackson was a bit crusty at first on the college football telecasts, but after five or six games he genuinely warmed up and became supportive.

With McKay, there was a palpable chill, beginning early in my genesis and continuing through on-air and off-air encounters. I surmised that he was concerned his stewardship of all the esoteric elements of *Wide World*, along with the real meat and potatoes—the national and international championships in track and field and swimming and gymnastics and figure skating—gradually might be inherited by someone else, perhaps a younger curator of "the thrill of victory and the agony of defeat." I wasn't close to that yet, but there was no one else on the announcing staff at the offices two or three times a week, reinforcing relationships with the people who might help one's career.

And in the 1970s and 1980s, most American sportscasting aspirants were looking to wind up in football or baseball, so it would have been crazy to have my kind of access to the most prolific provider of less conventional sports and not seek to capitalize on it. The fitness craze was at that moment reinventing Americans' views of their leisure time. And all that came together in one kaleidoscopic moment on the Kona Coast of Hawaii's Big Island at the 1982 Ironman Triathlon.

The triathlon as a competition structure was just gaining recognition. *Sports Illustrated* magazine had profiled the event—a 2.4-mile swim; a 112-mile bicycle race; and a marathon run, 26.2 miles—as first presented on the island of Oahu in 1978. The immediate outcropping of the article was that ABC Sports program executives bought television rights the following year for the 1980 edition of Ironman. Not having any eyewitness evidence to inform an opinion, the first step amounted to: "Is this real? Do human beings we've never heard of really swim more than two miles, then ride a bicycle more than a hundred miles, then run a full marathon back-to-back-to back?" As it turned out, they did.

In late 1980 I went to Oahu with a producer and director to create on handheld cameras ABC Sports' first pass at a telecast of the triathlon. Esoterica was nothing new, and we had introduced various lesser-known sports up to that point. A longer production time had been accommodated for coverage of marathon runs at the Olympics and in New York. What became awkward once the film had been edited and was ready to be narrated was that *Wide World* had for two decades been satisfying sports fans' desire for immediacy by providing as-though-live voice-over narrations for events that had taken place months before.

It was easy enough to defend that fiction with events that came in manageably small time increments. Ski races, logrolling competitions, wrist-wrestling matches, almost any *Wide World* staple could easily fit in an hour-and-a-half show with start-to-finish commentary that suggested it was live. Months after being in Honolulu, when I showed up in an enclosed audio booth at 7 West 66th Street in New York to narrate a competition that had been a nonstop, all-day enterprise, I wasn't shocked to be told by the producer that we would follow the *Wide World* tradition and call all this as though live.

It took a call to the coordinating producer, Dennis Lewin, and a lengthy urgent persuasion, and then another call up the ladder toward Roone, before I was able to get the point across: The event takes several hours, and in no way could we hide that, because it was the heart of the matter. We couldn't do justice to the triathlon and preserve the credibility of *Wide World* if we called it as if it were live. Only a documentary-style narration would work.

It was flummoxing at first to experience the kind of resistance that discussion incurred. But habits die hard, and the people in the *Wide World* cocoon were possessed by the notion that if we couldn't pretend it was live, their audience would rebel. I just kept pointing out the math: "The event takes up to 12 hours. It loses all its impact if we don't emphasize that. The program is 90 minutes on the air and viewers know that very well. We have no choice other than to do a documentary-style narration."

I won the argument, and we went forward toward a groundbreaking new adventure in *Wide World* programming. Ironman was the first true ultra-endurance sports event, establishing for the general sports public that human athletic endurance could stretch beyond the marathon distance of 26 miles and more. And no viewer complained that we didn't fake the timeline for the purpose of a supposedly live call.

Then in 1982, after the event was moved to the Big Island of Hawaii to create more room for the more than 300 swimmers who were now entering the water together, an unforgettable accident took the Ironman Triathlon to an explosive new identity in the culture, and it instantly transformed an unassuming California girl named Julie Moss into an everywoman hero.

The impact of the *Sports Illustrated* article had dramatically helped expand the number of participants from a dozen or so to more than a hundred. They were household names only in their own households, and most had a deep background in one—but only one—of the three disciplines they needed to master now. Many of them hired either a swim coach or a bicycling coach to get them to a more competitive level.

Moss, 23 years old, was a California college student doing research for an exercise physiology degree. With no previous major identity in that culture, she cruised through the swim and the bike ride and took a 10-minute lead among women headed toward the marathon finish in Kailua. Now with no more than a half mile left before the finish line, she collapsed from general fatigue and dehydration and was lying in the middle of a street, flopping back and forth on the hot pavement like a distressed fish.

Her body had evacuated fluids. The scene was graphic and self-descriptive. As the knot of observers grew around us, I sat in the camera truck while race officials loudly and repeatedly instructed the spectators not to touch her or assist her in any way because to do so would disqualify her. After several minutes on the pavement, Moss pulled herself up to a crawling position and began, haltingly and agonizingly, to move toward the finish line.

Spectators cheered and began rushing along the side of the street to try to get close enough to the finish line to see the climactic moment when she would break the tape.

And amid all that, another competitor showed up on the street. Kathleen McCartney had run the closing miles of the marathon course secure in the knowledge she was in second place, that another runner was somewhere up ahead of her, but if she could hold on she would be runner-up, which far exceeded her expectation. She didn't notice Moss crawling along on the street as she glided past her no more than 15 feet from the finish.

She stopped in momentary confusion in front of the tape, cognizant enough to expect that the tape was not for finishers other than the winner. As she looked down at it, standing still, a helpful official said, "Step through." Still confused, Kathleen followed his suggestion and broke the tape, thus becoming the women's champion of the race that from that moment forward would indelibly be identified in the endurance sports culture as "the Julie Moss triathlon."

It was well within the nature of *Wide World* that several months passed before the show was edited and ready to go on the air. During that period, an internal discussion at ABC Sports debated how that drama should be treated on the air. Inevitably, given the history of the show, there was talk that I might at some point come out of a commercial break dispensing with the past-tense docu-style narration on which I had stubbornly insisted and covered the closing segment as though live. I fought that battle and won it. From the moment Julie hit the pavement until after Kathleen broke the tape, we were silent, no commentary. I had never been prouder of my work. And amid totally unexpected attention and fanfare due to Moss's fateful collapse, the show got a rating dramatically higher than would ever have been expected by ABC.

And with that, a major new identity exploded into the world of endurance sports. The Ironman format was licensed and duplicated all around the world. NBC aggressively outbid ABC for the rights and heavily promoted its telecast as extreme endurance sports proliferated. They were doing the Tour de France, too, and the two events matched each other well as on-the-air properties. Ironman, utterly fledgling and mostly unobserved when we had first seen it, became a nine-figure global entity, hauling in hundreds of millions of dollars every year.

Julie Moss became, in endurance circles, a household name. Kathleen McCartney, an utterly graceful and generous soul from Julie's home city of San Diego, was the footnote in the saga.

Program planners at ABC Sports kept their ears to the ground to see if any other ultra-endurance events might yield such television drama. And while Ironman had dramatically expanded the general public's understanding of what extremes the human body could endure, there was something else on the horizon that would in fact dwarf it. The most extreme experience of my life would happen five times. It was a bicycle race from the Pacific Coast to the Atlantic, and its poetic title was the Race Across America.

———

The idea had first been incubated a few years earlier in the mind of an amateur Southern California cyclist named John Marino. He was seeking to create an American version of the Tour de France, and all his planning and organizing efforts had come together on the morning of August 4, 1982, at the Santa Monica Pier. Alongside living-legend distance swimmer Diana Nyad, I presented an opening on camera for a *Wide World* installment whose destiny was at least questionable, perhaps preposterous.

Marino and three other obscure but determined bicyclists came decked out in cycling gear and pointed east, in the direction of the Empire State Building in Manhattan more than 3,000 miles away.

A traveling team in a motor vehicle accompanied each rider, limited by strict rules about what kind of support could be provided. There was a prescribed map to New York City, encompassing every kind of surface from the hardwood of the pier itself to the asphalt of interstate highways to the soft dirt shoulders of some two-lane country roads.

Nobody knew for certain how long the trip would take because no one was sure it had ever been done. The only accepted certainty was that someone was going to do it now—ideally all four of them.

And ultimately, they did. But not before a series of surprises, not the least of which was that the race was led from start to finish by a hulking, seemingly ponderous farm boy from the cornfields of Illinois named Lon Haldeman. Marino and Michael Shermer, brainy academic types, and Olympic cyclist John Howard had updated, streamlined bikes and gear; they far more represented the image of Tour de France élan. Haldeman rode a larger, sturdier bike with noticeably fatter tires and a more gener-ous seat. You didn't at first expect him to keep up with the others, and you couldn't have been more wrong.

They left the Pacific Ocean behind in midmorning, and by sometime late that night, I found myself standing on a freeway overpass above I-10 near Blythe, approaching the border of Arizona, chatting with Halde-man's girlfriend and crew chief Susan Notorangelo. Innocently, I asked Susan: "When is Lon going to get off the bike for a rest?"

"Rest? We're going to New York. Aren't you going to New York?"

The question perfectly embodied the disconnect between normal, comfort-addicted people like me and those who had become swept up in what many of us referred to as the "fitness craze." From the beginning that day, the Race Across America was crazy, and compellingly so.

The following day I found a pay phone, called Dennis Lewin, and told him this likely would become an epic story. A week before, he had sug-gested to me it might be a 15- or 20-minute rundown on the air. Now, from somewhere in northern Arizona, I assured him that unless all four riders collapsed (and I didn't rule that out), it was going to be highly unusual and potentially gripping television. The most mundane details of daily life stretched across the outdoor canvas of a 3,000-mile nonstop bicycle race: Where and how to sleep? When to eat and brush teeth? How to deal with inevitable discomforts? Where to perform bodily functions?

There were four distinctly different personalities, and the one who had appeared cosmetically to be the least adept and well prepared was now the runaway leader. All of them were in their way compulsive, and we had one of America's most famously obsessive personalities, Diana Nyad, on the show. Nyad had begun her quest in 1978 to swim the 110 miles in shark-infested waters from Havana, Cuba, to Key West, Florida. She finally accomplished it on her fifth attempt at age 64 in 2013, later portrayed in a 2023 biopic by Best Actress Oscar nominee Annette Bening.

I told Denny: "This will be WAY more than fifteen or twenty minutes. This may even outstrip the Ironman Triathlon as an audience attraction." He was skeptical but intrigued. No one had expected at first that Ironman would inflame the culture the way it had. Now it was indisputably a future *Wide World* staple. This was weirder, less explicable, but it was clearly still an athletic competition.

I settled into my lawn chair in the back of the main camera truck and focused, hour after hour, day after day, on these four self-appointed guinea pigs. John Marino had shared with me that for years he had lain awake at night, wondering what it would feel like to ride a bike all the way across the United States, from ocean to ocean. On day five, riding past the arches in St. Louis, his bike shorts were crimson, soaked with the blood from his saddle sores. So now he knew. But to stop would be out of the question.

Haldeman made it to the Empire State Building in 9 days, 20 hours. John Howard, who had confidently declared himself the favorite in Santa Monica, was about 15 hours behind.

Michael Shermer was another 9 hours back, and Marino, without whose vision and determination it wouldn't have taken place, finally rolled into midtown Manhattan at 12 days, 7 hours and 37 minutes. A flag had been planted.

The program that aired a few months later on ABC was more like a feature film than a standard *Wide World* segment. In scripting it, I strove for understatement in every sentence, every word. The public response wasn't quite the emotional earthquake that Julie Moss's experience had produced, but it again pointed instructively toward the future: The ultra-endurance phenomenon was here to stay in the sports world and was being presented on *Wide World*. And for the moment, at least, the guiding narrative voice was mine.

Race Across America, which came to be known as RAAM, remained on *Wide World* through 1986. My career was expanding and proliferating in many different ways, but a lot of what I did repeated observations Jim McKay had originated and curated for two decades. This was something new, and as a television subject it belonged to Jim Lampley. So I was riding the crest of a wave I hadn't foreseen.

12

Optimistic Early '80s

C oming out of Lake Placid, and all through the summer into the fall of 1980, there was gathering evidence of my career momentum at ABC, along with new reasons to be seriously focused on how that blended with my personal life.

Joanne Mallis Lampley had delivered our first child, Brooke, on the night of March 30, 1980, at Lenox Hill Hospital. She arrived more hurriedly than expected, and as the delivery loomed, I was at work in Cambridge, Massachusetts, hosting *Wide World* coverage of the NCAA Swimming and Diving Championships at Harvard's Blodgett Pool. No one could have foreseen how appropriately auspicious those circumstances would be.

I was granted the liberty by the *Wide World* structure of recording several optional on-cameras with Mark Spitz and Donna de Varona, and since the event would be airing on a delayed schedule, we would be able to convene later in a studio to supply the as-though-live calls. That was all fairly common *Wide World* procedure, and just before midnight I held Brooke in my arms and rewarded her mother with a take-out cheeseburger from a diner on Lexington Avenue. Nine days before my 31st birthday I was a father. Like most everything else in my life at that point, it wasn't planned. It just happened.

My work at ABC Sports was a whirlwind. Though NBC and CBS were constantly engaged in the process of building their own anthology programs, they faced an uphill fight in trying to catch up to the identity and internal machinery of *Wide World*, which had been on the air since 1961 and had captured enduring rights deals with many of the most logical events for a sports anthology series. *Wide World* had also benefited from Jim McKay's voice and his signature opening narrative setup: "Spanning the globe to bring you the constant variety of sport: the thrill of victory, the agony of defeat, the human drama of athletic competition."

Now as my career was progressing, it made sense for my growth and exposure, and to McKay's desire for a more relaxed schedule, that I was the one who would "span the globe" via my travel schedule and try to fit in a personal life within the margins. Thus, my hasty marriage to Joanne, which had taken place on that April Sunday of 1979 when I was returning from London and the Rugby League Challenge Cup Final at Wembley Stadium.

That moment was a transitory marker of how rapidly my life was changing. Now, less than one year later, I was a father with a travel schedule that left most of the work of parenting on Joanne's plate. And in my heart, I knew we hadn't prepared for that and might not really be ready for it as a married couple. I had witnessed the copious divorce rate at ABC Sports; I already had one, and now, just turning 31, the beginning ingredients for a second. But our daughter was beautiful, so maybe she would provide the ballast necessary to grow our skimpy bond into a durable institution. It was worth hoping for.

I got a tacit but major vote of confidence going into the fall of 1980 when Roone Arledge reached out and hired Mike Pearl away from CBS to come into the studio and produce my *College Football Scoreboard*. Mike had overseen the development and execution of CBS's enormously respected and successful Sunday pro football studio wraparound, *NFL Today*. He had blended the panache of Brent Musburger, Irv Cross, Phyllis George, and Jimmy "The Greek" Snyder into a show that combined score updates and game previews with personality interplay and provocative information to significantly reinvent the concept of updating scores. A function that was previously seen as little more than a perfunctory formality had now become, under Mike's guidance, must-see sports TV. The suggestion that I would now be at the center of such an approach to college football was beyond thrilling for me.

We kept Beano Cook, who wasn't terribly dissimilar to Jimmy the Greek, and added Boston College's Heisman Trophy–winner Doug Flutie to the mix as the pregame, halftime, and postgame wraparound grew in significance and stature, and I grew with it.

By 1983 I had left behind forever the persona of the kid on the sidelines and the travel guide to obscure events and artsy adventures on *Wide World*. As Arledge and his lieutenants were making plans for the 1984 Winter Olympics in Sarajevo, and an expansion of on-air hours from an exotic Eastern European time zone, my agent, Art Kaminsky, was targeting the anchor chair and the beginning of a campaign to ease me gradually toward what he and I agreed was my best possible long-term identity at that network: successor to Jim McKay.

It was an audacious plan, which made it a worthwhile undertaking.

There was no point in shooting for any lesser target. With each step I had taken, from the football sidelines and soft features to the regional play-by-play booth to the studio wraparound, from Olympic personality interviews to the hard news reporting at Lake Placid, from the funky folklore of *Wide World* to national and world championship events in swimming and track and field, I had been gaining upward mobility in content terms. Now it was time to pay all that off.

McKay could not realistically host every meaningful on-air hour in Sarajevo. It was time for someone with similar skills to begin building stature for the future. And to Art and me, along with various producers and directors I had worked with, it was clear that someone was me. The arrival of Mike Pearl, and the unusual amount of money Roone had spent to bring him into the college football studio, was defining evidence in my favor.

There was to be a late-night show in Sarajevo, a live-and-tape combination of event coverage to follow the local 11 o'clock news. We plotted to go after that. There would be plenty of Olympics ahead to try for prime time. We began envisioning whom we would want on our team. Pearl was a given. His calm, confident presence in the control room was a safeguard for my studio presence on the college football telecast, and I knew Roone and his lieutenants felt the same way. But Mike had not been to the Olympics before, so it made sense for him to work with another producer who had. And that person was Dorrance Smith, my original feature producer on the sideline.

While Roone remained president of just the news division, it only made sense that some sports personnel would find their identities changing, and Dorrance was high on that list. He eventually became the producer of Sam Donaldson's Sunday show, and the combination of his linkage with me and his origin as a studio producer made him a no-brainer for the Sarajevo late-night team. I approached him, and he said he had already spoken to Roone about it.

So once the time arrived for Art Kaminsky to make our preference known, the correct control room team was on board. The next step was the selection of a co-host to collaborate with me. And that produced a highly ironic result.

The original expressed plan for the college-age reporter position was for a new talent hunt every year. By the end of the first season, Chuck

Howard had developed enough of a comfort level with me to tell Roone that ABC should bring me back in the fall of 1975. By that time, I was already blended into the *Wide World* mix, and then in 1976 I was given Olympics feature-reporter assignments at the Winter Games in Innsbruck and the Summer Games in Montreal. The whole organization was way too busy for anyone to go out on the road looking for a new college-age reporter, so the easy response in the fall of 1976 was to send me back out onto the sidelines. But with Dorrance Smith moving up, I needed a newly assigned producer from the younger troops to supervise my feature story shoots and be the liaison to Chuck in the truck during the games. And a new rising star was emerging within the organization.

Back in the Watergate summer of 1974, during the period when I was called to New York from Chapel Hill to interview for various jobs other than college-age reporter, I was included among a field of four for the chief 1976 Olympic research position. It was a job that bore an illustrious history.

The 1968 Grenoble and Mexico City research chief had been Dick Ebersol, who went on to be Roone's administrative assistant and then head of late-night programming at NBC, developing and overseeing *Saturday Night Live*. By 1983 I had every reason to think I would never be directly connected to Dick again, but I was wrong.

By the fall of '76, I was in my third year on the sideline. Dorrance had higher level production assignments, Jeff Ruhe was succeeding Ebersol as Roone's administrative assistant, and production assistant Ric LaCivita went to Howard to ask if he could become the Lampley caddie/supervisor that fall. I was delighted when Chuck said yes.

Ric and I became blood-brother-like best friends. After I moved to New York that fall we dined together, traveled together, watched sports events together, and Linda became the central adviser in his love life. She listened to his discourse on the women he was dating and offered feedback on how to do it right, ultimately providing critical assistance in his campaign to succeed a football star named Bob Baumhower as the love life focus for a graduating Alabama homecoming queen named Sela Ward, who went on to become a popular TV actress.

So it was fitting that when I reached the end of my comfort zone with the sideline reporter gig and wanted to make clear to Chuck and Roone that I was ready to leave that behind in favor of play-by-play for regional games, a way to encourage that was to suggest the team conduct another national search. And the team was Ric, Jeff, and me.

We cast a net with sports information directors and communications and journalism departments and went on the road. The three of us settled comfortably on only two candidates to recommend to Chuck and Roone. Both were undergraduate students at the University of Southern California. One was a ranking student political leader, a startlingly handsome senior named Alex Cappello. The other, equally impressive but in a different way, was a striking blue-eyed brunette named Kathleen Sullivan.

I thought either of the two could be at least as good as I had been. When Roone and Chuck either disagreed or couldn't decide, I was obliged, more or less, to go out for a third season of patrolling the sidelines, trying to make it clear I would be done with that gig after that. And I succeeded.

Now seven years later, as Jeff Ruhe, Mike Pearl, Dorrance Smith, and I were all planning for the late-night show in Sarajevo, Kathleen Sullivan showed up on the ABC radar again. She had already developed quite a career.

Shortly after graduating from USC, Kathleen had been hired as an anchor at CNN. I felt good that a visionary executive like Ted Turner saw in her what I had seen in our sideline search interview. Then, not too long after that, she signed a contract with ABC News. So when Dorrance and Mike asked me with whom I'd like to share the late-night studio at

Sarajevo, I was ready with the answer that was conveniently in-house. Roone went for it right away.

I had entered the Olympics picture as a fledgling feature reporter at Innsbruck and Montreal in 1976, then a much more significant news-based reporter at Lake Placid in 1980. And now, at my fourth Olympics, I would sit in a host chair for the hour-and-a-half segment that aired after the late local news. The time span was nearly 10 years from my first screening interview with Ebersol and Terry Jastrow to the planning sessions with Dorrance and Mike Pearl, but in some ways it felt like a few months. I was 34 years old, but anyone who knew me would have said I was a young 34, still boisterously immature and naïve to the ways of the corporate world in which I lived. But I was not so naïve that I didn't now focus on what was coming next.

The Summer Olympics in Los Angeles later that year promised to be one of the biggest shows in the history of ABC, and if things went well at Sarajevo, I would play a major role. It was astonishing. I was desolate about dropping out of college with a dead-end transcript at age 19. I could still see Eugene Terkoski's face as he urged me not to leave a menial paperwork job at First National Bank of Miami. I could still see my mother's tears as she told me all my father's air force pension money was gone, and if I was going to go back to Chapel Hill, I would have to pay for it on my own. I could still see my former father-in-law Jimmie Lee telling Linda at their dinner table she was out of her mind to be hooking up with a loser like me. And now I was going to help host the Winter Olympics on network television and had no doubt I was ready to be great at it.

13

Sarajevo and "Silent *Boléro*"

Lampley and colleagues let the music tell the story
(PCN Photography/Alamy Stock Photo)

A fter decades of Winter Olympics competitions in glamorous ski resorts like St. Moritz and Grenoble and Innsbruck, Sarajevo presented a striking cultural change. Part was due to the socialist politics of Yugoslavia, which tilted more toward the proletariat than those ritzy resort towns. Part was the product of Sarajevo's history, underlined by the singular event for which the city was most known: the political assassination in 1914 that touched off World War I.

At ABC we all learned going in that our headquarters hotel was where the Austrian Empire's archduke Ferdinand had slept the night before he was shot to death on a bridge in the middle of town—a bridge now colorfully named for his assassin, Gavrilo Princip. ABC Sports' chief logistics and planning officer, Marvin Bader, had trained himself for years to cater to Roone Arledge's worldly appreciation for the interfaces of history and culture, so it was critical to our identity that our organization occupied every room of the Bosna Hotel, the signature structure in the middle of town.

My close friend Jeff Ruhe was now fully installed as Roone's administrative assistant.

Partially because of that, and to some degree due to his marriage to Robert F. Kennedy's fifth child, Courtney, his suite above the hotel lobby became our elite social gathering place. The main floor dining room, which catered to foreign visitors, was also a party spot, and most of us ate all our breakfasts and many other meals in that environment.

Balkan beers and European wines flowed freely throughout the hotel. Because of the six-hour time difference between Sarajevo and New York, competitions were completed long before it was best to show them in the United States. And because this was decades before the internet, most American viewers were able to protect themselves from knowing the outcomes of events before turning on Jim McKay at eight o'clock eastern time. Little of our programming was live.

My wife Joanne was the Sephardic Jewish daughter of a garment salesman and his Turkish-born wife, both of whom were brought to the United States as infants to escape the persecution of Jews in Eastern Europe.

Joanne and Courtney hunkered down, ordered up a stream of Pouilly-Fuissé (a white wine) and french fries with mayonnaise, and welcomed guests from among the wives and visitors to the ABC Sports colony. Our four-year-old daughter, Brooke, was constantly attached to Joanne, and in terms of her day-to-day activity profile in Sarajevo, she might as well have been an adult, too. Just one of the girls, albeit no cigarettes or white wine.

None of them were candidates to don ski clothes and trek out into the snow to watch outdoor events at the alpine skiing or speed-skating venues. And their approach was validated when on the night of February 8, the day of the opening ceremony and the eve of outdoor competitions, nearly two feet of snow fell on Sarajevo and the surrounding mountains. That snowfall continued unabated for eight more days.

Jeff was enclosed in the control room and occasionally in Roone's office, helping to plan the ever-changing format for the prime-time show and seeing to it that Roone had a constantly updated information flow from which to work. Kathleen Sullivan and I went to the ABC broadcast center in midday and mostly sat in our own office and watched event coverage being taped for turnaround transmission to the United States.

Several times a day, Dorrance Smith and Mike Pearl cranked out a prospective format for our late-night show. Almost every newly revised version reflected the loss of some enticing program elements to the *prime-time show*. It became clear we might have to be inventive to be interesting.

By far the most prominent indoor competition was figure skating, despite the memory of the United States' gold medal triumph in hockey four years before. And from the beginning, much of the focus there fell on the charismatic and glamorous British pair Jayne Torvill and Christopher Dean. We began showing snippets of their practice sessions to pique audience interest, and the ratings suggested that was helping to keep late night afloat amid the sparse content availability.

It also helped that the first alpine skiing event was the men's downhill, and in a scarce circumstance, the favorite going in was an American from California named Bill Johnson. One month before the Olympic Games, he had become the first American man ever to win a World Cup downhill competition. The course on the Olympic ski mountain, Bjelnašnica, was flatter than most World Cup mountains and therefore offered an advantage to a proficient glider, a skier who could hunker down onto strong legs and maintain speed without the help of a steep incline. One applicable definition to Johnson's style, he was a glider. Even before the race, Johnson's European star rivals discounted the legitimacy of a gold medal if Johnson won it. After all, he had won only one World Cup downhill and was otherwise undistinguished. Afterward they were even more vocal once Johnson glided to victory through the heavy snow.

Kathleen was an enthusiastic cheerleader for Johnson, which was appropriate given that—as she pointed out—he had grown up just a few blocks from her home in the San Fernando Valley. She was already making a big impression on viewers in her new high-profile ABC Sports role, and her looks helped. Her strikingly dark hair was reinforced by the gray streak in her bangs, which framed her piercing blue eyes and electric smile. She was a formidable on-camera force, and she knew the language of sports well enough to present quite convincingly. Every time she talked about Bill Johnson, she had a small festival with the counterintuitive reality that the Olympic gold medalist in skiing's most prominent event, the men's downhill, was from "Van Nuys, California!"

In a news conference following his victory, a reporter asked Johnson what he thought might be the eventual spoils of his victory. No doubt thinking of how the Austrian and Swiss downhillers would capitalize on Olympic gold, he blurted out, "Millions, we're talking millions." But the eventual truth was that Bill Johnson lacked the positive personality and magnetism it would have taken for the American audience to celebrate a downhiller. At the end of the day, it was thousands, we're talking thousands. If any American performer could evoke a projection of "millions" based on the viewers' response in the first several days of Sarajevo, it was Kathleen. She was bursting onto the audience like a fresh-faced sensation.

———

I was just Jim Lampley, and ABC Sports viewers were now quite accustomed to me and my 10 years on the air in various upwardly mobile roles. So it should not have been surprising to me—though it was—that the first-week star of the late-night show in Sarajevo was Kathleen. The more press clippings I read, the more irritated I got, until Dorrance and Mike asked the press office to separate out some of her raves from my daily media response package. Which I quickly discovered, and which only irritated me more. Dorrance came into the office and reminded me I was the one with a full-time network contract, and she was only there for the Olympics. That helped. We moved on toward week two, as outside the window the snow continued to fall, every day and night.

Looking back, it's clear to me that the in-studio experience of Sarajevo was a preview of a problem that would later recur in my professional life. Accustomed from years of hosting college football and a lot of *Wide World* weekends to being in the studio chair alone, I had more trouble than any 34-year-old should have had with sharing that desk.

I realized in my heart I was strikingly immature about it, but outwardly I didn't want to admit it, so any time Dorrance or Mike would point out a way in which I had demonstrated my discomfort on camera, I was defensive and tried to wall it off. In my internal dialogue I wrote it off to Kathleen's extraordinary cockiness and self-absorption. Looking back, I think there might have been some of that in the mix, but it was smarter to view it as my own shortcoming.

If I had been smarter and more adept at dealing with it in Sarajevo, I might have been more effective at controlling my emotions the next time I was paired at an anchor desk with a skilled on-camera performer who projected glamorous poise and self-possession. But I did not see that coming in February 1984. I saw only my own storybook sideline-to-studio arc at ABC Sports, and I fully expected to pursue that on Roone Arledge's and Chuck Howard's terms for the rest of my television career.

And we were only five months away from a bigger series of telecasts at the Summer Olympics in Los Angeles. Art Kaminsky was assuring me that my performance in Sarajevo was well-received enough that I could look forward to another big platform in LA if I could just keep my head on straight. I buckled down for the second week in Sarajevo.

There was no American hockey story in Sarajevo to match the 1980 Miracle on Ice. Order was restored, the Russians went unbeaten and shut out the Czechs to win the gold medal. Sweden defeated Canada for bronze. National Hockey League players, regardless of nationality, were not eligible to play.

So, lacking an American hockey story, the second-week focus fell mostly on figure skating, at that point already the prime-time ratings bulwark of the Winter Games.

American success was helpfully provided by Scott Hamilton, who won the men's gold medal, and by Peter and Kitty Carruthers, whom I had met at Lake Placid and who won the silver medal in the pairs competition at Sarajevo.

Peter and Kitty were brought to the late-night show studio, and via my observations in the makeup room and on the set, I could see that Peter was just as bowled over by Kathleen's charms as millions of viewers were. When I commented on it, he said, "Where would I go to try to have a drink with her?" I took him back to the Bosna Hotel, sat him down in the overnight bar next to a delighted Kathleen, and left the two of them in their own silver medal celebration.

Later an East German teenager named Katarina Witt debuted before the American television audience and won the first of her two Olympic gold medals. But though Witt would go on to have perhaps the greatest 20th-century figure skating career, the true drama of week two in Sarajevo centered on ice dancing's Torvill and Dean. The global audience fell in love with the story and the skating of the former insurance book clerk (Jayne Torvill) and policeman (Christopher Dean) from Nottingham, England. They had been paired by an astute coach and had risen from a fifth-place finish at Lake Placid to become four-time world champions and prohibitive favorites for gold at Sarajevo.

Their signature long program was an athletic and romantic tour de force set to Ravel's *Boléro,* and on the night they nailed down the gold they achieved a near-impossibility on the ice, a perfect score. Words are insufficient to describe the level of drama the routine and their performance achieved, and the ABC broadcast center was electrified by the prospect that we could now promote on the network for hours in advance that the American audience was about to witness something that transcended figure skating, transcended sports in general, transcended entertainment.

In the late-night office, we were acutely aware that this would be the centerpiece of that night's prime-time show and would surely help draw the biggest rating of the two-week period. American women would see to that. And longtime ABC Sports viewers were accustomed by the network's programming history to the astute, often elegant commentary of Jim McKay and Dick Button. But we wanted to show the *Boléro,* too. So how to differentiate?

I'm not sure whether it was Dorrance or Mike who came up with the spectacular idea that elevated our late-night show to a place beyond anything we could have dreamed of on day one in Sarajevo. Now, six days later, brainstorming for a way to make this something other than a repetition of a great moment, it bubbled up in the office among the four of us. If it was my idea I would claim it, and if it was Kathleen's I would remember, so I am sure it was either from Dorrance Smith or Mike Pearl: Wipe the commentary off. Let the *Boléro* play for the TV audience exactly the way spectators experienced it in the ice arena. Just the music and the skating and the spontaneous bursts of cheers and applause and the breathtaking drama of it all.

As a four-person committee we signed off on that in seconds. Again, it was either Dorrance or Mike who said, "DON'T TELL ANYONE IN THIS BUILDING WHAT WE ARE DOING." That was brilliant foresight.

Among the newspaper writers who noticed it, the critical response in the United States was explosive. We had elevated something that by conventional expectations just COULDN'T be elevated. Among the rank and file in the broadcast center the response was the same. All day long for the next two days staffers from other assignments and workspaces showed up in our offices or the tape room asking to see the silent *Boléro*. If we had done nothing else singular in the two weeks of those Olympics, we had done THIS.

We got away with it—partly I am sure due to the critical response— but Roone made it clear that McKay and Button were not happy. What could he do? We had sneaked it over the transom. I'll be honest and acknowledge that if Roone had said anything to me about it, I'd have pointed to Dorrance and Mike. They were the producers. But McKay already harbored some negativity toward me, accurately observing my intentions regarding everything about him, including his Olympic chair, and the silent *Boléro* surely exacerbated that undercurrent.

And now late night in Sarajevo had something else to distinguish it in the minds of critics and the audience other than the stunning debut of Kathleen Sullivan.

Joanne Lampley and Courtney Kennedy Ruhe (and Brooke Lampley), sa-tiated by Sarajevo and eager to be back in Manhattan, had left after the first week, bonded for the future as best friends and lengthy lunch part-ners with Courtney's mother, Ethel Kennedy, at her traditional table just behind the maître d' stand at 21, next door to CBS on West 52nd Street.

Courtney was in love with the nickname—"Stacks of Wax"—Andy Sidaris had pinned on Joanne in the disco at Rex & Eric's in Hawaii six years earlier. "Joanne" was dropped, "Stacks" was permanently installed, and going forward Courtney and Ethel had a blast introducing my wife to upper-level government and society bigwigs as "Stacks of Wax." Joanne was thrilled by that, no matter how I felt.

For more than two weeks in Sarajevo I had occupied the office closest to Roone Arledge's, and he said that given what would be my long hours in the building—arriving in the early afternoon and waiting until the wee hours of the morning to go on camera with the show—I should regard myself as his personal guest and take full advantage of the stocked bar and humidor in his office. So I took him at his word.

I stayed away from his scotch and cognac and waited until we were off the air to have a morning beer or two on the way back to the Bosna. But there was so much time to kill, and I had never before allowed myself the privilege of a really expensive cigar. By the end of Sarajevo, I had what felt like a fully installed habit of smoking Davidoffs and Montecristos. And because they were Cuban, I couldn't buy them in the United States.

Marvin Bader, the longtime logistics genius, had a special relationship with a particular customs agent at John F. Kennedy International Airport. With Bader's help and approval, I altered my travel arrangement out of Yugoslavia to take me through Geneva, where in the airport shops I could gather dozens of Cuban cigars. Joanne would have no right to complain, given that some of her close friendship with Courtney was fueled by Winstons and Marlboros.

I spent a couple thousand dollars, maybe more, to get months' worth of cigars and a humidor that could in no way be concealed when I arrived in New York. The designated customs agent winked and waved me through, though I was nervous as the proverbial kitten. The agent kept a straight face, blessed the luggage without intervention, and asked me to say hi to Marvin next time I saw him. I boarded a limousine, sat alone in the back, and reflected all the way to the city on how privileged my life had become. I was a studio host at the Olympics, I had command of other studio chairs at ABC Sports, people were beginning to recognize me on the streets of Manhattan, my agent was counting up dollars to ask for in the next negotiation, and it would be some time before I had to worry about how to get ahold of the world's most coveted cigars.

I got out at 70 East 96th Street, watched the doorman haul my bags upstairs, and went inside to kiss my wife and daughter. Not too much later I unwrapped a Montecristo, clipped off one end, and lit it up, carefully opening a window in the living room so the smoke wouldn't accumulate. It was probably a few minutes before I admitted to myself it didn't taste the same.

Not the same at all. A couple of weeks later I took the cigars—almost all of them—to the office at 1330 Sixth, put them on the executive black market, and sold them at a discounted price. I gave the humidor to a doorman. In the 40 years since, I am not sure I have ever tasted another cigar.

Call it a statement on the exotic feel of Sarajevo, or the Winter Olympics, or Roone Arledge's office, or all three. It was just a different world.

14

Tinseltown Games

he next six months of 1984 went by fast, especially in the last week of June at the US Olympic Swimming Trials in Indianapolis.

I was already assured of a place in a play-by-play booth and in the late-night studio at the Summer Games in Los Angeles. In terms of collective audience and informational impact, they would constitute perhaps the largest sports event in American history.

If you had asked me at the beginning of the year what my dream assignment would be, I would have told you unequivocally I wanted to cover track and field (or as the Olympic structure now called it, "athletics").

I had the background for it, the information base, and familiarity with the athletes. I had covered more track and field at ABC than Al Michaels, who was the other reasonable choice, but from an overall perspective he was the more experienced play-by-play person, especially considering his dossier as a Major League Baseball voice. So that was one good reason not to be disappointed that Al would be at the Los Angeles Coliseum describing foot races and jumps.

The other good reason not to bitch about it, Art Kaminsky pointed out, was the schedule.

Swimming trials took place early in the morning. The finals were in the afternoon. Swimming was the only play-by-play gig that could comfortably pair with a studio host assignment, and I was once again ticketed for the late-night chair. But this time, to show Kathleen Sullivan to the audience for many more hours, she was paired with Frank Gifford in daytime. My late-night co-host was Donna de Varona, an old and dear friend who was, by her own admission, somewhat intimidated by the nature of on-camera hosting. She was also the expert commentator for women's swimming events, so we would be together from early morning to nine o'clock at night.

Everyone loved Donna, the two-time gold medalist as a 17-year-old at the 1964 Summer Games in Tokyo. There was no reason not to; she was by nature gracious, giving, unassuming, and generous. And we had known each other for 10 years so I knew she trusted me. That personality circumstance, along with the continuity I would enjoy with Mike Pearl and Dorrance Smith, made the late-night show in LA a breeze. The real bulk of my workload was swimming.

Because there were numerous preliminary heats for each event—men's and women's—in the morning, and then the finals at the end of the day as the sun was dramatically setting over the USC campus where the pool was located, the information demand was heavy. I had been calling swimming consistently on ABC since the week after the conclusion of the Montreal Olympics in 1976. My statistical brain was a swim-info fanatic named Bill Kunz, a Cal Berkeley grad on whom I relied for every plain fact and every somewhat hidden nuance.

Kunz had first earned his credibility with me when in 1976 at the US Swimming National Championships in Philadelphia, 10 days after the conclusion of the Olympics in Montreal, I had called my first live race on the air, taking over a chair that had belonged to Keith Jackson before me. I managed to call the men's 100-meter freestyle, establish the winner and the order of finish, and button it all up without noticing that the South African–born first-place finisher, a University of Alabama student named Jonty Skinner, had broken the world record in the event. My failure to notice that was, within the envelope of what we were doing, cataclysmic.

The producer, a *Wide World* veteran named Ned Steckel, didn't notice at first. We went to commercial time and began preparing for what would come next in the show. But at this point Bill Kunz spoke up and made clear we (meaning I) had just perpetrated an information disaster, and it needed to be fixed. And since the show was live, not taped, it would have to be fixed right away.

So Steckel quickly communicated to the US Swimming officials on the pool deck that we would need a slight delay before the arrival of the next race's participants on the starting blocks. We came back from commercial time with what amounted to me saying, "Oh, by the way, a meaningful element of the men's 100-meter freestyle you just saw . . ." and we replayed the swim, establishing that Skinner had set a record. From there it was on to whatever came next. It all happened so fast I didn't even have time to be thrown for a loop by it, and Bill Kunz just smiled and said, "Stick with me here, there's a lot of data to process."

Parenthetically, and by way of establishing the sometimes-astonishing level of coincidence in my life, I point out now that when I stepped away after 45 years of broadcasting and returned to the University of North Carolina in 2019 to teach a course I created, I was assigned a teaching assistant, a Communications Department PhD candidate named Kevin Alexander Pabst. Early in our association I learned he was a former University of Alabama swimmer, a breaststroker. Later I learned that his father had been the roommate of Jonty Skinner in Tuscaloosa in the middle 1970s.

I could not make things like this up. It happened—back in 1976. And despite the near-disastrous beginning, my arc as a swimming stroke commentator kept growing, so eight years later Bill Kunz and I were still joined at the statistical and biographical hip covering the world's most significant swim competition ever to that point in Los Angeles.

We benefited from the presence of producer Curt Gowdy Jr., who was the calmest, most precise and easy-to-work-with producer in the entire ABC Sports lineup.

And why not? The name said everything. He had grown up on the inside, his father was one of the biggest and most trusted names in the history of sports television and one of Roone's oldest and dearest friends, and his confidence simply couldn't be shaken.

Swimming was hectic, but Curt Gowdy Jr. was so calm he didn't even acknowledge "hectic." Donna, Mark Spitz, and I were lucky to have him, and we knew it.

The men's 100-meter freestyle remained the sport's most glamorous event, and the American story going into the LA Games was poignant. The most recognized and accomplished freestyler in America was Ambrose "Rowdy" Gaines of Winter Haven, Florida, and Auburn University. Poetically, he was the son of two professional Cypress Gardens water-skiers. He was now 25 years old and had represented the United States at two world championships and two Pan American Games. And he was the reigning world record holder in the event, but at 25 he was by the standards of his sport aging out.

We all knew Rowdy very well, probably better than we knew any other American swimmer at that point. He was universally popular, and for every good reason imaginable. I will never forget the unusually chilly late-summer night at the world championships in Berlin, Germany, in 1978, when from 80 yards away on the pool deck 19-year-old Rowdy Gaines had looked up to our outdoor announcer position and noticed that

I was shivering. He had climbed the stairs to the top row of that swimming stadium and gently, unobtrusively draped his US team windbreaker over my shoulders. As a human being, he was incomparable in his world.

Now, six years later, he was finally at his first Olympics. Of all the American athletes who had been martyred by the US boycott of the 1980 Games in Moscow, none was more painfully penalized than Rowdy. He might have won five gold medals there, when he was 21 years old and at his self-described peak. Now in Los Angeles he was 25, borderline ancient for the sport, and not considered a medal favorite in his signature event.

In fact, earlier that summer at the Olympic Trials in Indianapolis, our production team had prepared for the prospect of telling the story of his heartbreaking disappointment. Bill Kunz recited in our production meeting all the statistical information that powerfully suggested he might not finish in the top two and therefore fail to make the team. There was a catch in my voice when he reached the wall second behind Mike Heath, a qualifying position, and Spitz was similarly moved. At that moment, it was thrilling that the story lived. But there remained an undercurrent of dread. Clearly Heath was the more likely medal winner in LA.

So all of us were excited and apprehensive at the Olympics as we prepared to call the men's 100 free. But to be honest, more apprehensive than excited. There wasn't much good reason to think Rowdy would win. Entering the pool in Lane 3, he would be shoulder to shoulder with the overwhelming favorite, Mark Stockwell of Australia, and in setting up the field I focused on all the statistical information that buttressed Stockwell's status as the likely gold medalist. But I did mention that it was likely Rowdy Gaines's last race at this level, and that it would be painful if his career ended without an Olympic gold medal.

And then magic happened. In swimming it is called a flying start, the convergence of circumstances in which a swimmer somehow times the starting gun so that his body is pronated, his weight is moving forward, his arms are fully extended, his entry is in motion, but at the moment the gun sounds his feet are still touching the block. At the biggest, most propitious moment of his swimming life, Rowdy Gaines caught a flying start. He entered the water already in the lead, and from there swam a clean 100 meters, the only swimmer in the field to break 50 seconds, and he gave all of us at the pool a moment never to forget. Even the defeated Stockwell seemed thrilled for Rowdy.

On the pool deck afterward Rowdy told our interviewer, the great Diana Nyad, that his grandmother had dreamed it that way, and his coach had advised him that the timer at those Olympics was quick with the gun trigger, so "be ready." Beyond that, he was overwhelmed.

If you have the privilege of going to the Olympics with the host network, and I have 14 times, there are countless moments that stand out and will never be forgotten, but the most moving ones are based in a context of personal experience. Rowdy Gaines went on to win two more gold medals in Los Angeles, anchoring the freestyle and medley relays.

And every time we described him, I held in the back of my mind the memory of the teenage boy I had never met, who climbed to the top of a stadium in Berlin at a moment in the summer of 1978 when I was unexpectedly freezing cold. That's personal. That's special. That's Rowdy Gaines.

In the years since, his work on NBC Sports Olympics broadcasts has made him the most well-known swimming commentator and biographer of, among others, the incomparable Michael Phelps.

The late-night show with Donna was largely uneventful. The fact we spent so much of every day in each other's group made continuity and cooperation easy, and Donna had always been by nature a diplomat, even after first appearing on the cover of *Sports Illustrated* at age 14. In the world of sports politics and organization she had been a big and meaningful figure ever since her teenage years. She was the kind of person we wanted to send to meet with Peter Ueberroth, the LA Games organizer who later became commissioner of baseball. But live TV performance wasn't an area where she felt overpoweringly strong, and she trusted me. I treasure that.

For the live closing on camera of our last show, the producers articulated a scenario in which I started us off and pointed toward summary comments, then Donna would thoughtfully respond, and I would again pick it up and take a countdown to the off-air moment. A safe scenario, and Donna was happy. Then when we did it on the air, she was holding a pen in one hand. And as I approached the finish, she inadvertently dropped the pen onto our desk and it began rolling forward. I was at first only vaguely aware of the rolling pen until Donna reached with one hand to try to corral it. In our ears the production booth was counting down, "seven, six, five, four . . ." As the count reached the area of "two," Donna made one last stab with her now fully extended arm, and the pen fell off the front of the desk onto the floor. I turned to her and said "nice." And then the two weeks of the Los Angeles Olympics were over. Nicely.

———

For the audience and the world of sports, it was crucial that the United States and its many supportive allies around the world had returned to the fold after boycotting the Moscow Summer Games in 1980 to protest the Soviet invasion of Afghanistan. But the Olympic product of that boycott had been retaliation from the Eastern bloc and its allies.

The Soviet Union, East Germany, and Cuba were among the 14 nations that stayed away from Los Angeles. One of the sports most affected by that was boxing, and American boxers won nine gold medals, several more than would have been anticipated had Cubans, Russians, and East Germans been competing. I couldn't possibly have known at that moment how such a bumper crop of American boxing gold medalists would soon be figuring into my career.

I did notice, though, as did keen observers from the sports division's ranks, how angry Howard Cosell was at what he saw as underrepresentation of the boxing competition in the network's LA programming menu. He delivered an epic summary on the last day of the competition that decried the editorial choices of the control room in favor of other sports options, and that foreshadowed near-future changes in the network's approach to the ring.

It had been fun, and I was pretty sure we had done well. There is something about an Olympics set in an American time zone, where almost all the event programming can appear live, that makes it special. And I had no idea how important that LA time zone would eventually become in my life. But I knew my broad exposure at Los Angeles had again boosted my profile at ABC Sports, and I looked forward with some confidence to ongoing career progress there. I had a contract negotiation coming up, and Art Kaminsky was quite excited about it.

The fall of 1984 brought further solidification of the *College Football Scoreboard* as a division commitment, and after all the on-air hours in Los Angeles, I was more confident than ever in my studio hosting skills. I was also now traveling with the broadcast team of *Monday Night Football*, voicing the half-time highlights in place of Cosell, who had built that institution in his own image.

I realized from the beginning that was a thankless task, but at least I had someone to hang out with on the road. Director Chet Forte, Frank Gifford, and Don Meredith formed one social tier on that telecast. The younger tier was O.J. Simpson and me. On Sunday and Monday nights before and after the games, O.J. and I explored the bars and restaurants of America's NFL cities. If being identified with college football in college towns had presented one taste of glamour earlier in my career, this was another level up the scale. Ten years after I had first marveled at being friendly with him at the ABC *Superstars* show, I was inwardly marveling again. I was cooler now, but he was O.J. Simpson and still more demonstrably famous and high profile than the rising all-star players we were covering. He was royalty.

The new year in 1985 brought more studio airtime on *Wide World*, along with expanding profiles for the Ironman Triathlon and the Race Across America. I was beginning to develop a considerable legacy, and the prominence of my on-camera time helped Kaminsky upgrade his phone list. New possibilities were again coming into sight.

15

The Boxing Mistake

After the LA Olympics, Jim was in line to succeed Jim McKay
on *Wide World of Sports* (Courtesy of Jim Lampley)

By late 1986, and with my contract expiration coming up at ABC, Kaminsky informed me that he was again in contact with CBS, which was explicitly interested in my studio capabilities. That baffled me at first.

"I thought they were very high on Jim Nantz," I said.

"They are. That's not the studio slot they are talking about."

He made it clear to me he would not go further for the time being, and I realized he was walking a middle path between getting my hopes up unnecessarily and pointing out that I needed to keep performing impeccably. CBS didn't invest a lot of effort into fighting an anthology war with *Wide World*. This must have had something to do with the NFL, and their relationship with studio star Brent Musburger was known to be colorful. He had huge fame, recognizable talent, and it only made sense he would want much more money. I was making very good money, but not as much as Brent.

While I focused on minding my business, Art focused on maximizing the CBS interest one way or the other. I wasn't betting at that moment that I would steal the host chair at *NFL Today*. More likely I was going to use the specter of that to improve my circumstances at ABC. It would take only a few weeks to find out.

Art called and began to pick my brain. The essential subject was "How do you feel about taking a one-to-one meeting with Roone?" Simply, it was a high compliment that the most powerful and influential sports television executive in the history of the business wanted to see that, but if I wasn't inwardly secure enough to handle it well, it could be a dramatic pitfall. I understood Art's concern in that regard, and we kicked it back and forth for a couple of weeks.

Art's basic message was, "Don't think for a second he won't test your self-belief. He will. I have carved out a set of promises for him to make to you, and your role is to stand firm in the expectation of those promises.

He will try to get you to fall short, but they are promises that I have told him he must make if he doesn't want you to walk over to CBS. If you flinch, you will lose all the progress I have now gained for you, and it will be very difficult to get it back. Now if you trust what I say, and you tell me you are ready, I will go ahead and set up the one on one. Just you and Roone."

I was 37 years old and had spent the better part of a dozen years working on the air for the most prestigious sports television provider in the world. All my steps up the undeniably steep ladder there had been rubber-stamped by Roone. I was in the midst of a year in which I had ascended to being the host voice of the Grand Prix of Monaco on *Wide World*, the host voice of the Southern 500 from Darlington on *Wide World*, and the primary host voice of the whole month of May at the speedway in Indianapolis, climaxing with my call (alongside experts Sam Posey and Bobby Unser) of the Indianapolis 500.

Those had all been Jim McKay roles, and now they were mine (or so it appeared) if I could keep moving forward without applying "or else" pressure. He was Roone Arledge, and just under the surface I was still the kid from down the street in Hendersonville who had caddied at the golf course for his parents.

So I went to the meeting, acted like a grateful puppy, and failed to assert my right to all the tangible rewards Art told me Roone had already agreed to. I walked out with essentially the same circumstances with which I had walked in. And when Art called me for the follow-up, I all but bit off my tongue trying to avoid telling him the plain truth.

Pretty quickly he cut to the chase.

"Did you walk out with a promise of written specific contractual guarantees going forward for all the things we discussed? *Wide World* host, auto racing host, a tower on the golf telecasts, and the prime-time studio at the Olympics? He was prepared, according to what he told me, to give you all that in writing to prevent you from going across the street. Did you nail all that down?"

The answer was too humiliating to express in a simple declarative sentence. The shortest answer was, "No, but I don't think that's a problem. He knows what we want, and he assured me we will get it."

"Well, congratulations, Jim, you just cost yourself years of concrete promises I had lined up for you, and you have put yourself in a humiliating position. Now I must go through the process of rebuilding everything you tore down in there. So go home, sit tight, and try to learn from this. It gets harder and harder for me to take care of a client who doesn't seem to want to take care of himself, but rest assured I will earn my living. I know how."

"Did I totally ruin my career?" I was bereft. I knew Art basically loved me, but he wasn't trying to make me feel better.

"No. The fact is your career has become too good to ruin. They know who you are, they have built you, they can't afford to lose that investment to a competitor, and Roone will follow through on the things he tacitly promised to me in the buildup to this. You just have to suffer a little more humiliation because you asked for it. Now go home and keep your head out of the oven. This is a misstep, but it will be okay. Trust me, they can't afford to lose you."

Eventually, I signed a contract that specifically included all the career steps Art had been working on, all the stair-step promises Roone had avoided in our face-to-face. Most significantly, the contract laid out moving toward succeeding the great Jim McKay in his Olympics chair. With the Winter Games in Calgary less than a year and a half away, that was a visible, tangible career reality almost too good to be true.

As it turned out, we can remove "almost" from that sentence. In the suddenly changing world of network television, it was indeed too good to be true. After CBS Sports boss Neal Pilson hired that smooth, young broadcaster Jim Nantz to host their college football telecast, it was clear that Art and I had missed something in the tea leaves.

My new contract was one of Roone Arledge's last concrete acts as president of ABC Sports. For two years, I had been paying little attention to an ongoing transition that would begin to reshape and redefine my television sports commentary career. Not long after my meeting with Roone, he stepped away from ABC Sports to devote full focus to his other job as president of ABC News.

That seemed on the surface to be logical because if president of sports was a full-time 12-hour-a-day job (and it was), president of news was a full-time 24-hour job. As the news division developed more and more programming under Arledge, the network's nightly news telecast, *World News Tonight*, had surprisingly risen to number one in the ratings race. That success had massive implications for the image picture and the profit picture at ABC. I assumed the growth of his news division was the primary reason Roone was leaving Sports. But I didn't see the entire photo.

ABC, owned by one man, Leonard Goldenson, from its start 35 years earlier, was now in the process of being acquired by an aggressive stations ownership group, Capital Cities Broadcasting. I knew a little about them since they owned one of our stations, and I was contracted full-time to the national entity, the network. But stations, if properly managed, earn money 24 hours a day, and Capital Cities had grown affluent enough to buy a network by doing a great job every day running its stations. And the company moved into its new perch with a clear picture of what it wanted to do.

An executive named Larry Pollock, who had built ABC affiliate WPVI-TV in Philadelphia into the most profitable station in the country, took over the division that ran network-owned stations. To make that move, Capital Cities was bumping Pollock's predecessor to the network and made clear to the most successful manager in the building that he wouldn't be allowed to keep running two divisions. And the company gave Roone Arledge a choice.

Overseeing EITHER Sports or News was an overwhelming job in and of itself. Predictably given their respective significances, Arledge chose News. Soon after that, it was apparent the real motivation was freeing up the sports division for the executive who had been running the owned stations without robbing him of prestige.

The new president of ABC Sports was a Midwestern ex-marine named Dennis Swanson, who brought in a significantly different view of his division.

The merger was completed in January 1986. Executives whose working lives were entirely devoted to amping up the profits of stations in medium-size cities entered the building on Avenue of the Americas to begin controlling network programming. Since it was an entirely different business, most of us thought they would need a period of adjustment.

Suddenly, the man I was pretty sure I had never met sauntered in with one hard-and-fast predilection: "Who is Jim Lampley and why are we paying him all this money?" Swanson asked.

All that took place shortly after Art's rescue of the contract promises that made it worth my while to deflect any planned defection to another network. I didn't see Dennis Swanson coming, and I'm pretty sure Art didn't either. But as 1986 had turned into 1987, somewhat out of my sight at first but eventually as plain as day, every day, the new ABC Sports president made it clear that he didn't care in the slightest what his predecessor might have promised me. He didn't care about the language in my contract. And he PARTICULARLY didn't care about a pathway for me to ultimately succeed Jim McKay as the Olympic anchor.

Swanson told Kaminsky, "That just isn't going to happen. Not on my watch."

As promised, Swanson set about seeking to make my life uncomfortable. He had made it clear to my agent he had no intention of honoring my contract, and that he would find ways to offload me before the 1988 Calgary Olympics. After 12 largely uninterrupted years of gradual upward progress, I was in shock. Arthur advised me to settle in, focus on each show I was doing, and see if the weather would change. I had more than two years left on the contract.

And as Art pointed out, Swanson's intentions in my regard were so overtly obvious that it made sense to suspect the Capital Cities executives knew his plans all along. I spent a few months chafing in place and waiting for the weather to restore the kind of golden good luck I had been accustomed to through all of my ABC years. Wouldn't my guardian angel, Chuck Howard, be able to turn Swanson around? Nope. Chuck was given an imposed retirement and sent bewildered to his Westchester home in Pound Ridge.

Wouldn't the various television sports columnists writing for publications like the *Daily News* and *USA Today* come to my rescue? If Swanson was willing to cashier Howard and could get away with that, there was no way he cared what the perpetually curious Rudy Martzke was writing in *USA Today*.

I was keeping my mind alive by throwing myself whole hog into the role of introductory biographer for the half dozen stars with new medals from the boycott-blessed Los Angeles Olympic boxing competition, and they had been contracted in bulk to ABC.

At the same time, my career had expanded in a different direction. A savvy Indianapolis entrepreneur named Jeff Smulyan had purchased the time-honored license of WNBC-AM in New York for the purpose of exploring an adventure in the rapidly growing field of talk radio: a 24-hour sports talk format, the first of its kind. Kaminsky sat down with Smulyan and convinced him to hire me as the linchpin talk show host for the station, commanding the prime daytime talk slot and voicing most of the station's introductory promotions. And I became the first daytime signature talk show host for the newly renamed WFAN. It seemed like an overmatch but was right on target in the zeitgeist of 1987, so I had an instant audience.

On Thursday, July 1, 1987, I went to Astoria Studios in Queens and at 10 AM eastern time officially put WFAN Radio on the air. Within the first hour of that radio show, working from notes I had created the night before, I issued a series of outlandish observations about all the different ways this new medium would permanently alter the sports landscape: that listener/callers would create fantasy trades, offload players from the teams they followed, hire and fire coaches, transform franchises, sell them and buy them on the air.

And in various fashions in various American cities over the next several years, all those predictions came true; 24-hour sports talk took off like a nickel rocket from day one and continues to stir the pot to this day. For a week or two, I thought it would be the backbone of my new career. But Kaminsky was fielding television offers now.

And that was emotionally indispensable because a few weeks later, I walked into 1330 Sixth Avenue with Arthur and formally signed the documents that spelled out ABC's downwardly revised obligations to me. To be real about it, in boxing terms, I threw in the towel.

I was already scheduled for interviews with other networks, but in my way of thinking, I would likely never again rise to the level where I had worked for nearly 13 years. When I bitterly expressed that to Art, he took me firmly in hand.

"Listen. Get over it. You might have 40 years to go in this business, so don't fly off the handle and blow yourself up. After all, Swanson took your job. Just your job. He can't take away your talent."

With those words, in that moment, my eventually-to-be-beloved agent saved my career and my life. And he was just getting started.

———

What happened next was one of the most significant accidents of my career—or you might say of my life. As a vehicle for making me uncomfortable, and to purposely make me look bad on the air, Swanson chose to assign me to boxing. He knew I had no background covering it. Until a few years before, no announcer type would have mentioned the word in the building because Howard Cosell called boxing and he did it by himself, no expert commentator.

That was Howard's way of controlling that turf. But in 1983, Cosell had sworn off professional boxing on the air during his call of Larry Holmes's too-easy bloody win over Randall "Tex" Cobb. In the two intervening years, various ABC announcers had called fights—Keith Jackson, Al Michaels, Don Chevrier, there might have been others—but no continuing ringside identity had yet emerged. The last thing on Swanson's mind was that I might become that presence.

I had always been a fan, going three decades back to 1950s fighters like Sugar Ray Robinson and Dick Tiger and Carmen Basilio, and I was obsessive about Ali and Sugar Ray Leonard and Thomas Hearns. But Swanson had me typecast as a silver-spoon East Coast type who would be allergic to boxing and would find it would be allergic to me.

So, without consulting me, I was on the assignment sheet for upcoming boxing matches, in an announcing partnership with the executive who for several years had been our division's liaison to the sport. He had negotiated fight contracts, built and maintained relationships with promoters and managers, and gone to places much grittier than 21 and P.J. Clarke's. His name was Alex Wallau, and Swanson might not have been paying attention. Alex was exactly what he erroneously perceived me to be: a silver-spoon type from Greenwich, Connecticut; except Alex had an inexplicable lifelong obsession with boxing.

At that moment I was living in an apartment on Madison Avenue between 93rd and 94th streets. Alex lived on Fifth Avenue less than 10 blocks north, between 102nd and 103rd. It was a 12-minute walk. Just hours after learning of the assignment change, Alex summoned me to his living room for boxing video clinics. More than 35 years later I am a permanent member of the International Boxing Hall of Fame, and I can tell you I owe a huge portion of the credit for my ringside credibility to Alex.

He showed me how inside fighters look to hold the opponent on the side opposite from the referee. He showed me how in the battle between the conventional fighter and the southpaw, control often belongs to the fighter who can keep his front foot on the outside of the opponent's front foot. He showed me that musculature bears no relation to power, that sometimes willowy, skinny fighters can knock you into next week and sometimes prison-buffed bodybuilder types can't crack an egg. He put me through hours of training to prepare for our first show together, a bout featuring an unknown teenager ABC had signed named Mike Tyson.

"Jim, you're only 38 years old," my agent reassured me. "When one door closes, another one opens."

And so it did. Purely coincidentally, but as a separate outgrowth of the same kind of management politics that had now conspired against me at ABC Sports, there was a small earthquake erupting among the CBS-owned-and-operated stations in Los Angeles. The sports director at KCBS-TV, a popular and energetic former pro football player named Jim Hill, was taking a massive monetary offer to move across town to

KABC-TV. His move would likely rock the ratings meter in the nation's second-largest local TV market, which by the way was seemingly certain to surpass New York and become the largest.

I knew little about the monetary impact of local stations. I had spent 13 charmed years in the rarified air of the undisputed number one *network* sports division. I had been taught and conditioned into an attitude of snobbery that viewed local sportscasters as lesser creatures. I had rubbed shoulders with Cosell and McKay and Gifford and more recently Al Michaels. To accept a demotion to fronting the nightly sports summaries for a local audience at 6 and 11? Why would I even consider it?

Kaminsky was blunt: "What you are blithely ignoring is that the contract Jim Hill is walking away from at KCBS-TV is larger than your deal with ABC Sports, and the new deal he is getting at KABC-TV is larger still. The CBS-owned stations division wants to talk to you right now, and they have already cleared the path for you to have an accompanying deal with CBS Sports, so you will still have your precious network status calling NFL games and maybe even college basketball games.

"And they will carve away a portion of the exclusivity to allow you to call fights on HBO, just in case that opportunity should arise. It's a spectacular offer, so if you're willing to contemplate it, the KCBS-TV news director, Erik Sorenson, will fly here to meet with you. Say yes to that?"

By now I had lived in New York for a little more than 10 years. My impulsive marriage to Brooklyn-born Joanne Faith Mallis had given me two beautiful daughters and a constant stream of personality-driven headaches, conditions that might possibly benefit from a change of scenery. And though HBO hadn't yet tendered an offer, I knew the executives were considering it now that Mike Tyson had emerged to become the acknowledged heavyweight champion by the World Boxing Council (WBC).

And WFAN signaled that it loved the idea I could do the daily four-hour talk segment built largely on New York sports topics via satellite from a studio in Los Angeles. If Kaminsky's vision was to be fulfilled, I would have several jobs each with different contracts, and I could laugh myself to sleep at night thinking of all the money I was making after Dennis Swanson forced me out at ABC Sports.

"Will I make seven figures?" I asked Art.

"Easily. You'll have everything but leisure time. And you've already proven you are a workaholic. So when do you want to sit down with Erik Sorenson?"

And now, to go on the menu with KCBS-TV, CBS Sports, and WFAN Radio, Art was deep into negotiations with HBO. The pay-TV channel had solidified a relationship with Tyson, and it wanted me to come call his fights, along with many of the other most prestigious matches in the sport.

The sport that Dennis Swanson had chosen as the vehicle to publicly embarrass me into leaving my original network TV home was about to become, in my estimation, my most prestigious pedestal yet. I had preliminary conversations with Seth Abraham, the president of HBO's sports division, and then deeper, more detailed discussions with the executive producer who ran the boxing telecasts, Ross Greenburg. In addition to the boxing matches, I would host and call HBO's weekday telecasts from the All England Lawn Tennis Championships at Wimbledon every summer. I would work at ringside with Larry Merchant, whom I had long idolized, and Ray Leonard, who had become a good friend. And, I was to find out, I would work at tennis matches with the immortal Arthur Ashe.

16

Cosell and Me

One of the traits that set Roone Arledge apart from his executive competitors at CBS Sports and NBC Sports was his gift for finding sportscasters with unique personalities distinct from those who caused television booths to feel homogenized and predictable. "The kid on the sideline" was surely an example of that, but there were numerous others.

Roone hired Bob Cousy as an NBA expert even though he had a speech variation that showed up when he arrived for his first show. Arledge hired the brilliant Billie Jean King, though she was anything but a natural and at first seemed startled to be on the air.

By far the most radical find was a hyper-ambitious Scarsdale attorney named Howard Cosell. Looking back, I think it's fair to say he was the first sportscaster in America to break the barriers of the sports world and cross over into general cultural stardom. He pursued fame via his verbal duels with Muhammad Ali and became the centerpiece for Arledge's highest-impact programming innovation, *Monday Night Football*. To a greater degree than any other sports broadcaster up to that point, Howard (identifiable by first name only) didn't just appear on the shows, he *was* the shows.

The story of how Arledge discovered Cosell and chose to shine light on him was an inside ABC Sports legend. Roone's first big network job was in children's programming at NBC. On Saturday mornings in the back seat of his limo to the NBC studios in Rockefeller Center, he would tune in to the local Little League baseball radio show Cosell had created on his own. The folk fable about their broadcast arcs never cleared up for me what role, if any, Arledge played in hoisting Cosell from the world of Little League baseball in Westchester County to big league sports on ABC Radio. By the early '60s that elevation had taken place, and by the mid-'60s the playfully combative give-and-take with Ali on ABC was renewable week after week.

In the first few years of my tenure at ABC, I had virtually no interaction with Howard Cosell, whom I later found out was born in North Carolina. I was involved in college football, not the NFL.

There were visible ladders to climb, and every year there were new potential stars to observe. In boxing the new faces seemed to come out of nowhere, which made them more exotic. The storyteller at first was Don Dunphy, and later there were others, including Tim Ryan and Barry Tompkins and Marv Albert, who helped guide my path to knowledge of the ring before I ever got near a ringside chair. And for the first 13 years I worked at ABC Sports, there was Cosell, and boxing was his other personal franchise.

To say Howard was protective of his boxing turf is an understatement. He worked individually, with no expert commentator, the implication being that he was the expert, and he effectively projected that he was on a different level than other blow-by-blow announcers. He did this by establishing with words and body language that he was closer to the fighters, more intimately associated, and therefore more authoritatively knowledgeable than anyone else could possibly be.

Cosell and Me

It was a craft, and Howard was so good at it that most fighters instinctively played along.

I saw it at work with Muhammad Ali, and he continued it with Larry Holmes and George Foreman and Ray Leonard and Tommy Hearns and Marvin Hagler. They might sometimes appear on other networks, but Howard managed to imply that those occasions were exotic excursions to lesser exposures. Their real homes were at ABC, under his wing. It was such an effective schtick that it went largely unchallenged, and though I gradually crept into his world—as the first successor to his voice on the *Monday Night Football* half-time highlights—all I got was the clear understanding that to follow his path in any way would be career suicide.

———

On one or two occasions when I visited *Monday Night Football* telecasts and sat in the production truck right behind Don Ohlmeyer, the producer, and director Chet Forte, if Cosell stepped in, he ignored me.

And I wasn't alone. Ohlmeyer, a Notre Dame alumnus with inborn swagger and precociousness for command, and Forte, a former Columbia basketball All-America who as a senior averaged 29 points a game, had hugely healthy egos and charismatic auras. Howard couldn't intimidate them. But people like me, with less imposing backgrounds, had every reason to be fearful of Cosell. He was blustering and dismissive, sometimes venal, downright antisocial around those he saw as lesser mortals. Seeking his approval was a losing game.

I wasn't thinking in terms of opportunity when I learned in the early 1980s that ABC was going to satisfy a Cosell demand for his own news and feature reporting show on Sundays, a program to be called *ABC Sports-Beat*. Howard would produce and host the show, which would be billed as cutting-edge sports journalism at a level only Howard could reach. And it turned out that was indisputably true, if you happened to believe the most relevant stories every weekend involved studio interviews with any of four close Cosell cohorts: Al Davis, owner of the Oakland Raiders; George Steinbrenner, owner of the Yankees; baseball commissioner Bowie Kuhn; and Sonny Werblin, the wealthy entrepreneur whose extensive tentacles ultimately touched seemingly everything in New York sports, including the Jets, the Meadowlands Sports Complex, Madison Square Garden, the Knicks, and the Rangers. As Cosell loved to call him while he waited for his friend to arrive for their frequent lunches around the corner at 21: "David A. Sonny as in money Werblin."

Those four sports titans—Werblin, Kuhn, Davis, and Steinbrenner—rotated more or less equally into the guest chair in the *SportsBeat* studio, but to balance the show another element was required: a field reporter, someone who would get on a plane and go somewhere Howard didn't want to go for information and interviews relative to a subject that could be seen as sports journalism. A 28th-floor decision established that role would be mine. And along with it came a new office space, on the 12th floor where *SportsBeat* was now set up. I was just a few doors down a hallway from Howard. And soon I learned what he was doing with most of his time in the office: writing his memoir books, some of which turned out to be scathing in their depictions of his *Monday Night Football* and executive-suite colleagues. But at first not many people had an intimate view of what would be in the tell-all books.

It was shocking when suddenly I did. It surely wasn't the product of any affection he harbored for me. In retrospect, I would cite the simple fact that I was a captive audience. To amuse himself during afternoons following what Werblin himself described as "the three-martini lunch," Howard would send a secretary down the hall to summon me into his surprisingly small enclosure. Then the great man would open his drawer, pull out the recent galleys from his series of books: *Like It Is*, and the one that would most get Roone's attention, *I Never Played the Game.*

Cosell would motion me into a chair facing him across the desk and proceed to read the latest written material out loud. My role was no mystery: I was there to tell him his perspective was unmatched, his perception of issues and interrelationships equally outstanding, and the publication of this next book would take his reputation to entirely another level. And Howard not-so-modestly agreed.

Then I would go back down the hall to my office and wait to hear the review. He would emerge from the office and stand amid the three secretaries, audible to his old friend and executive producer Ed Silverman, sometimes to brilliant fledgling feature producer Alexis Denny, and speak loudly enough for me to hear. There were variations on the theme.

Good review: "You know, the kid, Lampley, is the only other one here who is capable of completing a coherent sentence under pressure. He's no genius, but at least he can speak the language. He won't embarrass us like any of his *Monday Night Football* or *Wide World* colleagues, as he could eviscerate them all, even the great Jim McKay."

There might have been more complimentary material, but the above is what I vividly remember. My conviction was that he didn't mean a word of it. Because at least as frequently I received a bad review. "You know, Lampley is an embarrassment to ABC. A sophomore, hired, promoted, now being paid a six-figure salary, it's ridiculous. Thank God I have the unique vision to know how to use him here, but the more those idiots on the 28th floor expand his exposure to the public, the more dangerous he will become."

Cosell was Cosell, and from him I got pretty much what I expected. It wasn't friendly, but it was visibly theatrical and insincere, so I brushed it off. I was an oddly acquired character, ironically somewhat like him, with his ongoing public and personal drama, and though he made it clear it was absurd that I was taken seriously in the halls of 1330 Sixth Avenue, he felt no need to seriously attack me. To do so would have been an indirect attack on Roone, and Howard would never do that.

Since all I ever offered in return for the book readings was gushing praise, I usually had no idea what prompted the attitude of the office soliloquy. Nor did the secretaries or Alexis Denny or Ed Silverman. It just was what it was. When I had the brutal one-year experience of replacing him as the voice of half-time highlights on *MNF*, I was aware of his scorching derision. Fortunately, by the time I began calling boxing matches in 1987, his clock had finally run out, and whatever the review of that was, I never heard it. Or, in hindsight, maybe I did.

Less than a year after I left ABC, I was exploring guest possibilities for a new syndicated interview program that would air on CBS stations, the title of which was *One on One with Jim Lampley*. The format allotted 20 minutes per subject, and I had attracted Carl Lewis, Chris Evert, and Wayne Gretzky, and now, since *SportsBeat* had dissipated, I was somehow consumed with the vision that Howard Cosell would provide the perfect balance for the track star, the tennis starlet, and the hockey star. I still had in my address book his apartment phone number in Manhattan.

"Hello?"

"Hi, Howard, it's Jim Lampley. How are you?"

Silence. I gathered he was in shock. I had never used the number before. I plunged forward with a description, as brief as I could make it, of what I wanted. After a pregnant pause he answered in characteristically stentorian tones, the volume steadily escalating in his delivery.

"Are you kidding? Are you completely out of your mind? You want me to embarrass myself and my own incomparable image to service the needs of your drooling ambition? You are a prime example of all the worst things that go on in the craven business of sports television, and it embarrasses me already that I was ever associated with you in any way at all. You'd sell your own grandmother to succeed. NO! Now go away and leave me alone with my dignity."

Okay. I hung up. I guess he didn't recall my groveling after the galley-listening sessions in his office. Or maybe he did and just disrespected the opportunism that was visibly apparent in my sucking up to him. Or maybe it was that I had just signed a contract to do boxing on HBO, which had now become the center of the sport. Whatever it was, that was the last contact I ever had with Howard.

I would never be so self-congratulatory as to say he didn't positively influence me. As a reporter and defender of what he saw as truth, he was matchless and in some ways the best example of how to resist corruptive institutional influences. As a human being he was productively insane, waking up at 6:30 every morning, no matter how much vodka had been consumed the night before, scared to death someone else might read the *New York Times* before he did. As a sports broadcasting personality he was unusual, though you can now see many imitations in the relentlessly imitative world of cable television sports programs. Some of them sound a bit like Howard when they are breathlessly chasing a topic in hopes of being quoted on social media. But none of them is the giant of verbosity and insecurity Howard Cosell was. He invented what they do, and then on the way out he shattered the mold in self-defense. It was the only brand of defense he ever would have played.

17

Tennis: The Ashe Effect

"Two of the Best I Ever Worked With" (Courtesy of HBO)

O f all the sports I played badly as a pre-teen and onward from there, none was more frustrating than tennis.

I could throw okay, so I found things to do in football and

baseball for a while, before my basic absence of strength slammed my threshold into my face. I inherited enough of my father's noteworthy golf skill to be number two on my high school team, but it was a working-class high school. I wouldn't have been number two at nearby archrival Coral Gables, and I knew it. I was horrible at basketball (weak, small hands), and my one year of swimming with my age group mostly proved I was no fish, in water or out.

So as my career developed at ABC Sports, and Roone Arledge's lieutenants exercised due diligence to determine how I might be useful, I wasn't directing them toward tennis. That was fine because there wasn't much of it on the network. Wimbledon aired on NBC, and the US Open was on CBS. Those were major championships. When ABC Sports covered tennis in the 1970s, it most frequently reflected Roone's flair for show business. The Robert F. Kennedy Pro-Celebrity Tournament at Forest Hills was classic Arledge, and the Battle of the Sexes between Billie Jean King and Bobby Riggs was even more so, and in both cases, as with a lot of ABC Sports items you would identify as "classic Arledge," the host and principal narrator was Howard Cosell.

Still in my 20s, still most widely identified as "the kid on the sidelines of college football," still alternating between pinching myself to see if I was really a network television sports commentator and cursing under my breath at the indignity of being sent to cover the lumberjacks or the wrist wrestlers for the third or fourth time . . . and still well short of the audacity it would take to succeed Cosell as the *Monday Night Football* half-time highlights voice, I gave not the slightest thought to seeking exposures in tennis.

Striking, because I was becoming friendly with Ethel Kennedy, who was still involved in the RFK tournament, and that stays with me to this day. But, generally, there was no legitimately famous person in the world with whom I could possibly exceed the connection Howard enjoyed with them. In my sparse assortment of contacts with him, he made it clear he would see to that. So for various reasons, no tennis.

Then in the mid-1980s, the WCT Tournament of Champions came to Forest Hills, several years after the US Open had moved to a sparkling new facility a few miles away in Flushing. By this time Cosell, piqued that the network had canceled his personal sports journalism vehicle *SportsBeat*, had left television behind. So, at a moment when Arledge was looking to elevate my profile, I was assigned to host ABC coverage of the tournament, and though I was fearful, I was delighted that the expert commentator would be Arthur Ashe.

Because my mother had gifted me with an intense devotion to the goal of racial justice, I had followed Arthur Ashe's career. I knew about his development and upbringing on Blacks-only tennis courts in Richmond, Virginia, his barrier-erasing NCAA championship at UCLA, his US Open championship in 1968. That was for years the crowning achievement of his career. But he shocked the world seven years later when he cerebrally mastered heavily favored Jimmy Connors in the 1975 Wimbledon Final. I would be honored to meet Arthur.

In 1986, I went with less trepidation than was merited to do live stroke-by-stroke tennis commentary. Looking back, it must have been a distracting moment in my life. Early on in exchanging commentary with Arthur, I began committing the cardinal sin of tennis commentary: speaking over the on-court exchange. He flashed a couple of curious looks my way as we observed a few games, then in the commercial break he spoke directly.

"Hey, have you done tennis before?"

I wasn't exactly Bud Collins. Whatever I said in response, it was determinedly noncommittal. After the initial shock of being called out, I grasped the concept and set about trying to find the rhythm. But to be honest, there was no reason at all I should have been sitting in that chair at that time. I knew how to keep score, and I had absorbed all the bio information and knew some stories on the surface, but most viewers knew more than I did. Arthur generously covered for me for two days, Saturday and Sunday.

A year after I had left ABC Sports and was piecing together a new set of relationships, HBO Sports executive producer Ross Greenburg acknowledged to me that one of the talents his network saw in me was that I could cover tennis. Who knew where he had gotten that impression. No matter what I really thought, I ardently agreed and made a mental note to watch tapes of someone who knew how.

———

I signed my first contract with HBO in early 1988 and became host of the Wimbledon presentation that June. Because I had a day job at KCBS-TV that occupied my time prior to the flight to London, Wimbledon was a preparation challenge. HBO's deal was to broadcast five hours of coverage on weekdays. That meant I was in the chair five hours straight, welcoming and dispatching experts from subject to subject throughout, calling men's singles or women's singles live or on tape, identifying and describing players from among a day-one draw of 256 men and women. No amount of rehearsal would prepare me.

Following the pattern I had established doing the Tournament of Champions on ABC with Arthur and Billie Jean King, I got better, letting the sport speak mostly for itself and erring on the side of dignity. That first summer led to my being designated by *Tennis* magazine as the worst television commentator in the sport. I learned enough going forward never to be so identified again.

Take away my tennis illiteracy and the sport was perfect for me. The telecasts were five hours, eventually six hours, no commercials. A considerable portion of the job was to generate and sustain a conversation with the experts around me—at first mostly Ashe and Billie Jean, but as time went on also Martina Navratilova, John Lloyd, Barry MacKay, and Mary Carillo. Mary was a creative conversationalist, which was invaluable on the days—not infrequent—when rain would convert the telecasts to six hours live, no commercials and no tennis.

Those shows were still worth watching if Mary was involved.

The experts on the set were Arthur and Billie Jean. In whatever your walk of life, I applaud your spectacular good luck if you have ever found yourself similarly situated with regard to character, intelligence, substance, and accomplishment. I began every day at Wimbledon that way and stayed in that place sharing their company and their friendship in 1988 and for four more years before Arthur died young. And in those five years I got the gift of seeing one thing intimately and clearly: that Arthur Ashe was the most diligent and productive human being I had ever met. He gave more of himself to every minute than anyone else I had ever known.

Arthur was not a commentary genius. He was far too studious and polite and decent to achieve that. But he was adept at seeing through players' facades and interpreting their competitive reality for us. One day in 1990 he and I were in rapt attention watching Goran Ivanišević, the dominant southpaw laser server of that moment, as he was building a breakout semifinal win over three-time champion Boris Becker.

At age 18, Ivanišević was coming off the quarterfinals round on clay courts in Paris. Now his extreme velocity serves were skidding off the grass like rocks skipping on a mountain lake. He won the first set 6–4 and reached 5–5 in a second set tiebreaker, two points away from a two-set lead. Arthur had been quiet. Just as Ivo extended downward to set up his first serve, Arthur said, "You know, he hasn't had a single double fault all day."

And 60 seconds later he had his first double fault. I was impressed enough by that moment of clairvoyance to just remain quiet and wait to see what he would say next. Ivo extended and Arthur whispered, "They often come in twos."

Bang bang, another double fault; Ivanišević was perturbed enough to be undone now, and after four sets he was, and Becker moved on to another final. Later I asked Arthur how he had seen that coming so clearly and definitively, and there was no explanation beyond the obvious. The combination of Arthur Ashe's accumulated wisdom and Ivanišević's stage of progression in tennis life had made that moment of TV commentary magic inevitable.

But far more than commentary magic, Arthur was about human magic. In those years he was writing newspaper columns, including a daily piece in London's *Independent*, he was raising global awareness of apartheid, associated issues of racially based disadvantage, later AIDS, youth tennis, and other crusades. He also was coaching formally and informally, personally advising several of the ATP Tour's aspiring stars, and totally devoted to his wife, photographer Jeanne Moutoussamy-Ashe and their daughter, Camera.

Camera Ashe was a few years younger than my eldest daughter, Brooke, who was born in 1980. On long car rides to and from the Athenaeum Hotel every day, Arthur and I shared all our tales about the joys and discoveries of parenting. Once Arthur discovered he had contracted AIDS from a blood transfusion associated with his heart bypass surgery back in 1983, those conversations bore an ominous undertone. Arthur was frank about the limitations of his hopes and dreams.

One day between matches in the announcing booth, we were discussing the subject of my two daughters' travels back and forth from London, where their mother was now living, to Los Angeles to see me. Offhandedly I asked Arthur, "If you could have complete control, where do you think you would most want Camera to grow up?" I was thinking of his truly global connections.

"It's funny you should ask that. Jeanne and I were discussing it over the weekend, and I suspect the answer will surprise you." I was accustomed to that. Just the day before he had educated me, despite his stringent opposition to apartheid and the way that defined South Africa for him, that Capetown was the world's most beautiful city, and there was no reason to even attempt debating the point.

"I'd want to bring her up in Richmond."

"What? You did everything you could to get OUT of Richmond. When you arrived at UCLA you swore it off."

"I know. I can't deny that. But at the end of the day, it's the place that made me who I am. I'd want her to feel the things I felt there and respond in her own way." As it turned out, Jeanne was from Chicago and New York, and she would wind up being the one to choose where Camera was raised.

I went to Wimbledon 12 times, from 1988 to 1999, and spent much of that time covering the arcs of Pete Sampras and Steffi Graf. They were historic players, and the memories I harbor from covering them are rich. But by far my most treasured experiences at Wimbledon were the deep and instructive friendships I formed with all the brilliant and classy people who occupied that booth. I mean . . . I got to be close friends with Arthur and Martina and Billie Jean and Mary. It's a privilege far beyond words.

Within the first few days of that experience in 1988, watching how Ashe kept himself busy every moment of every day, I realized I had never seen a more productive man. As soon as we would finish taping an on-camera or the call of a match, Arthur pulled out a legal pad on which he was writing an editorial for the London *Independent*, or a legal brief related to the ongoing fight against apartheid in South Africa, or a document for his foundation supporting minority athletes, particularly tennis players, in the United States. There was seldom an idle minute.

It wasn't until 1992 that Arthur, having been tipped off that news media organizations had become aware he had contracted AIDS from a blood transfusion relative to his treatment, finally opened up and reluctantly shared his reality with the world at large. Reluctantly, because Camera was still growing up. Back then, AIDS was almost a medical death sentence, and it was revealed that Arthur had known about it since early 1988, just a few months before we first worked together for HBO, and I had begun marveling at his determination to never waste a minute.

I suspect that was a factor in what I saw. But not the primary factor. The primary factor was the basic nature of Arthur Ashe.

Arthur died suddenly of pneumonia on February 6, 1993, the same day I called Riddick Bowe versus Michael Dokes at Madison Square Garden, where the death was announced to the crowd. The example Ashe set by publicizing his AIDS and pushing for the development of drugs that would come too late to help him is an object lesson in humanity and has already outdistanced his spectacular tennis career as the defining mark in his story. I have known no greater man.

———

To be in that world every summer at Wimbledon in the rarified company of our living legend expert commentators, and covering historic figures like John McEnroe, Ivan Lendl, Sampras, Andre Agassi, Graf, and the Williams sisters was a rare privilege even in a life now blessed with various irrational privileges. And even after 12 years of it, I was still just learning how to call tennis matches.

I was getting to know Larry Merchant well via my contact with him on the boxing telecast, and Larry was also assigned to Wimbledon as a feature reporter and essayist. One day in the sedan that took us back and forth from the Athenaeum Hotel in London's West End to the All England

Club in Wimbledon, Larry regaled me with the story establishing Arthur's importance as an athlete. It related to something I had watched on commercial TV in 1975, Arthur's epic upset win over Jimmy Connors for the Wimbledon championship.

For the three decades after the arrival of Jackie Robinson in Major League Baseball, as Larry described it, there was an unspoken understanding between American sports media and its consumers that the triumphs of Black athletes could be seen as the product of physicality. The reasoning went that Black athletes were generally stronger, faster, quicker, even more coordinated than their fair-skinned counterparts, and that accounted for their success.

Public expression of that attitude had significantly diminished in the decades since writers like Jack London had openly called on heavyweight boxer Jim Jeffries to come out of retirement and perform as the "Great White Hope" against Jack Johnson. But it remained in the residue of American sports culture, and still affected public attitudes toward sports—almost all sports—as they became increasingly dominated by the exploits of Black stars.

Even so, it would have been difficult for any objective observer, even a skilled and qualified sportswriter or commentator, to make the case in 1975 that Arthur was in some way physically superior to Connors. To even the untrained eye it was inescapable that Connors was faster, hit the ball harder, had greater physical skills, and was in no way athletically inferior to Ashe. Realistically, the only way Ashe would beat Connors on a fast grass surface would be to outthink him. And so he did.

Inspired by the thoughtful competitive script he had watched Muhammad Ali create against George Foreman in Zaire the year before, Ashe blunted Connors's knockout power by playing around it and past it. He chipped volleys to Connors, making Jimmy reach, mostly to his forehand side, frustrating his power by constantly taking speed off the ball, swinging Connors constantly from one side of the court to the other. It was a masterpiece of tactics and strategy.

It was BRAINY, and the following day even ardent white racists had to admit in private conversations that the Black player had thoroughly outsmarted the white superstar.

I had watched it, but in 1975 at age 26 I lacked the perspective to see the sea change that it was. In a conversation 13 years later at Wimbledon, Larry Merchant spelled all that out for me. And now I was getting the privilege of working with Larry on HBO Boxing, too.

In the middle of that first Wimbledon in 1988, Larry and I boarded a flight from London to JFK and took a limousine ride to Atlantic City to cover the heavyweight title unification fight between Mike Tyson and the smaller, more experienced, more cerebrally tactical Michael Spinks. In a vivid reminder that in some cases brute force does in fact carry the day, Tyson knocked out Spinks in 91 seconds to claim the WBC, WBA, and IBF titles as the lineal world champion.

Just a few days short of his 22nd birthday, the youngest heavyweight champion in history looked for all the world as though he might never lose. But as subsequent events in his lifetime and mine would establish, that's always a mirage.

18

Mike Tyson and Me

"Mike Finally Found Happiness" (Courtesy of Will Hart)

BC Sports, motivated by Alex Wallau's relationships, had signed a contract with the 19-year-old heavyweight punching phenom from upstate New York who, while growing up, had exposure to gangs and drug cartels but managed to escape that life. Mike Tyson would beat journeyman Jesse Ferguson in Troy, New York, on February 16, 1986.

This would be Tyson's first fight on broadcast national television since the Olympic trials as an amateur.

In our meeting with Mike the day before the fight, he was markedly soft-spoken and polite. He hugged Alex coming in, as did some members of his posse, so I was the outsider in the room. Alex asked most of the questions, and for his part Mike acted genuinely 19, kind of uninformed, and in a way tender. Alex explained to me that Mike was superbly managed by Jimmy Jacobs and Bill Cayton, two old pros who knew exactly what they were doing, and they were grooming him for the maximum in global exposure.

The following day Mike created a spectacle, just as Alex had told me and the network he would. In the fifth round he broke Jesse Ferguson's nose with a perfectly placed uppercut, and a round later Jesse was bleeding so profusely that he was disqualified for holding. In a classic moment of career building, Cayton and Jacobs got the New York State Athletic Commission to change the DQ to a TKO, to preserve Mike's career-beginning knockout streak. In the post-fight interview with Alex, Tyson gave a hint of his near-future niche as the most prolific quote machine in sports. Alex asked about the classic right uppercut that had wrecked Ferguson.

"Cus D'Amato taught me the purpose of the uppercut is to drive the opponent's nose bone into his brain, so that's what I was trying to do, I wanted to drive the nose bone into his brain. I knew I could finish the fight." Indeed.

Calling the fight hadn't been at all uncomfortable. Working with Alex was a dream, he was so inside it all. Tyson had a storyline built around the bid to become history's youngest heavyweight champion. I began to consider that I might just have backed into a good parking space. But I should have kept the car running.

In his next ABC fight on May 3, Tyson's 19-straight knockout streak ended as the crafty James "Quick" Tillis took him the distance in Glens Falls, New York. I knew the knockout streak wouldn't last forever, but I still felt disappointment. I now understand, better than I did then, there are professional techniques for avoiding being knocked out, and veterans like Tillis know how to use them.

Seventeen days later, Mike had his first fight at Madison Square Garden. The opponent was a former amateur star named Mitch "Blood" Green. Like Tillis before him, Green was taller than Tyson and had some defensive skills. Again, Mike was given a decision, this time wider than Tillis's scores, but the large crowd at the Garden was disappointed, expecting fireworks.

The Green fight was on a local New York channel, not on HBO, so since I would have the night off from a microphone, Art Kaminsky talked me into inviting Dennis Swanson to be my guest at the Garden. To my surprise he accepted. We knew Swanson was dickering over whether to compete with an expected contract bid by HBO to try to hold on to Tyson's rights. By the end of the dull fight, it was clear to me from the division president's body language that Mike would be headed out the door. I wasn't quite sure if I should follow him.

The last Tyson fight on ABC was set for July 26, 1983, again upstate in Glens Falls. The opponent was Marvis Frazier, who was trained by his father, Joe, and had been irrationally rushed three years before into a title fight against heavyweight champ Larry Holmes, which ended in a first-round knockout.

Alex Wallau kept a beautiful green Jaguar in a garage near his apartment, and by now we had developed a routine for the Tyson upstate scenario, which meant Alex programmed the music, Alex picked the route, and Alex drove us back and forth, stopping for food at Alex-history diners along the way. It was a pleasure, and when he wasn't introducing me to obscure rock and roll groups like Cock Robin, he was always talking boxing, and I was absorbing this like the proverbial sponge. And while he was the authority on boxing, he made it clear he regarded me as the authority on what to say on TV.

"Lamps, I have a serious question."

"Sure. What?"

"Do you think I should predict in the opening on camera that Mike will knock Marvis out in the first round?"

"Well, that has to depend on whether you believe it. Are you certain of it?"

"Couldn't be more certain."

"Well, Alex, you are the expert. If you think that is the best way to illuminate the matchup, that's what you should say."

"Okay, that settles it. I'm going to predict a first-round knockout."

Silence. Back to music for a while. Then nearly an hour later, music off.

"What would you think of me predicting he will knock him out in the first minute of the first round? One-minute knockout, what do you think?"

"Alex, it's all about what you believe. It would be very attention getting, and as long as Mike does knock Marvis out, I don't think anyone will penalize you for it."

This was before the internet, before social media.

"Aah, I don't know for sure," Alex said. "Feels pretty audacious."

I teased him. "Nothing ventured, nothing gained."

Another half hour of music. Then the last volley.

"I'm going to go with the first-round knockout."

He seemed satisfied. It was brave enough and had two more minutes of margin for error. The one-minute knockout prediction went by the wayside.

In the ring, Marvis looked uneasy. Then Tyson landed a huge uppercut, followed by a combination. Referee Joe Cortez began to count, then looked closely and waved his arms. Marvis was out cold. Thirty seconds on the nose.

All the way back to the city Alex ranted at himself. "Why didn't I have the nerve to say what I really believed?" I couldn't convince him the first-round KO prediction was good enough. He couldn't have been more depressed. He felt like he had left money on the table.

———————

At that point in his career Mike made the sensible move and migrated to HBO. At that time the logic was less visible to the average sports fan than continuing history would show. ABC appeared in every television home in America, while HBO was still developing and only a minority of households were anteing up the monthly fee for what was mostly seen as a movie-recycling channel. The high-impact drama series like *The Sopranos* and *The Wire* that later came to identify HBO's artistic profile were not yet in development. But the network, along with its direct competitor Showtime, saw a pathway to growth in boxing.

The critical link was boxing's entrepreneurial nature. While major sports like NFL football, Major League Baseball, and NBA basketball thrived on abundance and regularity, boxing matches were more like popcorn movies—they came along once, they would never come again in exactly the same form—and if you missed them there was no certain chance you would see those two fighters live in the moment of confrontation. If the Bears lost to the Packers in September, there was a guaranteed rematch coming up in November. But in boxing you had no guarantee that Ray Leonard and Marvelous Marvin Hagler would ever meet again. And as history demonstrates, they didn't. So every major fight was the Super Bowl, which made it the perfect sport for premium pay cable.

I remained at ABC calling fights with Alex and collecting on the contract Swanson was determined to destroy. I was still the studio host of college football. I was developing a portfolio in a new genre of extreme endurance events, which were winning awards for originality and inventiveness. And the contract that included the critical guarantees for marquee exposure at the Calgary Winter Olympics was still there in black and white. Until my agent decided that was untenable.

On Monday, June 28, 1987, I got a call from Kaminsky advising me that before the end of that week we would be summoned to a meeting in Swanson's office at which I would agree to resign from ABC Sports.

"Jim, he just isn't under any circumstance going to honor the contract in Calgary. Very shortly the publicity process will begin and it will immediately become clear to other media you are being stiffed. You could sue them, but it would be an insurmountable black mark on your career image. There are only three of these networks, and while that implies competition in many ways, they operate as a cartel. You sue one, you sue them all. We're not going to do that. You go in, you shake his hand, you walk away honorably, and we'll see what CBS or NBC have to offer. It's not the end of the world."

To me, it felt like the end of the world. Hadn't I been publicly anointed by the great Roone Arledge? I had. But looking around me, I knew that already a significant number of ABC Sports stalwarts with Arledge-blessed identities had been rooted out: the head of production who ran college football, Chuck Howard; Roone's handpicked administrative assistant, Jeff Ruhe, who was now safely married to Ethel Kennedy's daughter Courtney; star producers Terry O'Neil and Ric LaCivita; all these people close friends of mine, now elsewhere despite their histories. I was just another chess piece to be removed from the board. I wasn't a pawn, maybe I was a rook or a bishop, but I was being taken out.

It felt like my precious career was being erased. Art said again, "Jim, he is taking away your job. He can't take away your proven talent. That stays in place."

On July 2, I walked out of ABC after nearly 13 years. By the end of the year, I was living in Los Angeles where I was sports director for the CBS-owned station there. I had a prime-time interview show titled *One on One with Jim Lampley* that aired on CBS four times a year. I was calling CBS

Sports telecasts of NFL games on Sundays. I had a daily three-hour slot on the pioneer station for 24-hour sports talk radio, WFAN and was already making twice as much money as I had earned in the ABC contract I had left behind. And most significant, I was signing a new contract to become the voice of boxing and Wimbledon at HBO, where Mike Tyson had become the youngest heavyweight champion in the history of prizefighting before taking his first loss in a huge upset to Buster Douglas on February 11, 1990, in Tokyo.

———

The Tyson narrative was built and rebuilt until it was interrupted by his 1992 conviction and incarceration for rape. That was a weird experience for those of us at HBO who had never had to deal with the cognitive dissonance of having a friend or a business associate charged with rape. I slept restlessly over the three years Mike spent in prison and was relieved when he was released. When friends asked me what I thought about his guilt or innocence I just said, "I was not on the jury, so I'm not equipped to judge."

The Mike Tyson I dealt with in the years that followed was always civil and congenial. I owe him a form of gratitude for being an eye-catching and galvanizing subject in my career.

When in 2002 HBO and Showtime made an unprecedented partnership deal to put Lennox Lewis into the ring with Tyson, I was chosen to call the fight with Showtime's Bobby Czyz. After Tyson ran across the stage and bit Lennox's leg at the initial press conference in New York, a vagabond tour was conducted to find a city and a state boxing commission willing to host the event. The promoter Main Events wound up with a deal in Memphis on June 8. In boxing terms, Tennessee was not Nevada or New York or New Jersey, but Tennessee it would be.

There was no fighter meeting the day before the bout because Tyson wanted no part of it. I rehearsed a few things with Czyz because we had never even spoken before, much less traded comments during a fight. It was agreed that our pre-fight on-camera appearance would conclude with each of us predicting who would win. Czyz picked Tyson, which I judged to be in line with Showtime politics. I had been telling radio audiences for years that Lennox Lewis was a larger, stronger, much better version of Buster Douglas, whose style had given Tyson his first loss in Tokyo 12 years before. I had been scoffed at by radio hosts and callers all that time.

I also knew that two decades before that night, when Mike and Lennox were teenagers, Lennox's amateur coach, Arnie Boehm, had taken his pupil from Kitchener, Ontario, to the Catskills to spend a week with Tyson and Cus D'Amato. The boxers worked out together and watched old black-and-white fight films on a white sheet draped against the wall in the room where they slept. Mike told me that at the beginning of the week Lennox seemed tentative and intimidated, but by the time Lewis left to go back to Canada, he was more than holding his own. So I was confident when I picked Lennox to win on camera. I had it, symbolically, from the horse's mouth.

The fight was just as one-sided as I had expected. Lennox controlled Tyson with his jab and gradually began to mix in power shots. Lewis's trainer, Emanuel Steward, was still properly respectful of Tyson's one-punch power and fretted in the corner, sometimes cursing his fighter for, in his view, getting too careless. Lennox flashed a little grin and urged him to calm down, suggesting that he was playing with Mike, having fun with him. When Lewis wasted Tyson once and for all with a savage right cross in the eighth round, a truly great handheld cameraman named Gordy Saiger leaned out over the ring ropes to focus downward on the supine Tyson, and his lens revealed blood seeping from Tyson's mouth, from his nose, from the tender flesh around both eyes.

In the post-fight interview in the ring, Lennox was joined as he almost always was by his mother, Violet. Mike was overwhelmingly gracious, praising Lewis for his dominance, documenting that they had known each other since boyhood, professing love for Lewis and his mother, even reaching across interviewer Jim Gray at one point to gently clear a globule of blood—his blood—off Lennox's cheek. It was beautiful. It was love. It was the height of what sets prizefighting apart from other sports.

The pay-per-view fight over HBO and Showtime set a record with 1.95 million purchases at $55 each, a gross of more than $107 million, which has only been eclipsed since then by four Floyd Mayweather fights.

Before Tyson was knocked out by Lewis in the eighth round, I had not had a face-to-face conversation with Mike since a ringside interview at the Alex Stewart fight exactly 11 and a half years before. HBO wanted me to go to his dressing room to see if he would have a longer conversation on camera, to sum it all up. Throughout the weekend in Memphis, a few of Mike's fans and followers confronted me, knowing that I had spent years denigrating his level of competition and predicting his demise against Lennox. Some of those closest to King and Tyson had openly threatened me.

"Hey, Mike knows the bullshit you been spreading about him. You'd better not bump into him in a dark hallway."

His dressing room was in a dark hallway. There were three very large men in black suits and bowler hats standing near the door. I asked one of them where I could find Mike. He smiled and pointed to the door. "Go on in. I think he's expecting you."

I found Mike Tyson sitting alone on a metal chair in the middle of an empty room. On his lap was a naked baby boy, whom I later identified as his son Miguel, the first of two children he had out of wedlock after his tumultuous two-year marriage to actress Robin Givens ended in divorce. Mike was gently stroking the infant as he sat quietly. Not sure how to treat this, I waited for him to set the tone. Without looking up, he delivered an opening line I couldn't have possibly imagined.

"I've missed you."

And in that moment, I realized that didn't refer just to me. He missed the glory of his pre-prison HBO days. He missed the legitimacy of being the real heavyweight champion of the world. He missed the luster of HBO. He missed all the things he had sacrificed on one lost weekend in Tokyo. He missed being Mike Tyson. Then the follow-up:

"I didn't have a chance in there. What did everyone expect? He's six feet, six inches tall. I'm about five ten. I couldn't have reached him with a baseball bat."

There would be no interview. I just wasn't going to put him through it. I had known him, at first up close, later from a distance, for more than 16 years. And at that moment, I saw a larger, wiser, more humane person than I had ever seen before. For the first time I felt I was getting a clear picture of Mike Tyson. I left the room overwhelmed with admiration for him. He had grown up, mostly on the strength of his own bitter experiences, and as the baby on his lap portrayed, he was still capable of love. Maybe more capable than ever before.

Over the ensuing two decades, I have seen Mike many times, and because of his more recent emergence into a different public persona, it won't shock anyone to know he has been uniformly gracious, polite, respectful, and a true friend, not just to me but to everyone else I know who has the privilege of knowing him. To people from outside the boxing culture I always say, and Mike has affirmed to me, "The old image of the Baddest Man on the Planet, that's not Mike. Not by any means. The shy kid on the rooftops building relationships with pigeons? That is Mike, to the core."

When he was the loneliest of lonely boys, choosing to stay away from the gangs, the pigeons made him happy. His greatest victory as an adult is that through a hard path, he found a way for his life to make him happy. That is a championship worth winning, and it fills me with joy to see that he has won it.

19

Pay Cable on HBO

Merchant: "Boxing Is Theater of the Unexpected" (Courtesy of Will Hart)

A ll through my childhood and well into my teenage years I rev-
eled in watching boxing on television. I saw the metamorpho-
sis that ultimately took the sport away from the Gillette Friday
Night Fights and moved it to *ABC's Wide World of Sports,* and then to

Wide World's anthology competitors, *CBS Sports Spectacular* and NBC's *Sportsworld.*

I watched as boxing's multiethnic panorama became broader and more diverse than those of the conventional, less entrepreneurial sports like football, baseball, and basketball. I'm not saying those sports did not gradually welcome and showcase non-white athletes, because they did. But only boxing had Sugar Ray Robinson, only boxing had Emile Griffith and Yama Bahama and Benny "Kid" Paret. Only boxing had Cassius Marcellus Clay, who of his own volition and determination became Muhammad Ali. Only boxing had Manny Pacquaio.

In boxing more than in more conventional sports, I saw athletes charting their own paths toward identity and stardom and potential wealth. In 1986 boxing was the last thing on my mind at ABC. Dennis Swanson was right about that. And by that point it was crystal clear boxing distribution was irreversibly headed away from the three major commercial networks. It was a process that had germinated 16 years before but was only now coming to fruition.

The pivotal event in the 20th-century evolution of boxing television was the Fight of the Century, Ali-Frazier I on March 8, 1971, which was piped into arenas and theaters all over the country. Because of its explosive sociopolitical impact and the dramatic personality contrast it presented, Ali-Frazier more than any fight before or since underlined and embodied the difference between major boxing matches and games of any kind.

Boxers don't "play." They bring their lives to the ring in whole cloth, and those lives are altered in front of the audience in real time. And because the entire enterprise is inescapably subjective, sometimes the official result falls in contrast to an emotional result for the audience. So Joe Frazier won the Fight of the Century, and yet it was Muhammad Ali who got bigger.

So going forward, the point had been made: The key to profit for boxing was not the breadth of the audience that wanted to see a fight, but rather the size of the audience that would pay a significant user fee. Their intense desire was the heart of the matter. Boxing would wind up going to media that employed a user-fee model for establishing access, replacing network television.

No, not every fight would be Ali-Frazier. Not even close. But for the same monthly fee that got them movies on TV, and the original programming that HBO and Showtime so creatively developed, sports fans who bought the premium pay-cable networks would get boxing, too. And if the human stories were told effectively, the sports would fit neatly with the surrounding programs.

When HBO and Showtime arrived and evolved, their event delivery model was not likely to displace the long-established norms of conventional commercial televising of football, baseball and basketball. It just wasn't a choice the NFL, NBA, and Major League Baseball were likely to make, given all the money they had been fed for decades by advertiser-based TV.

But in boxing, every event was a snowflake, and every athlete was an entrepreneur. So the marriage made sense on several levels, and as premium pay-cable TV matured through the '70s and '80s, boxing found its footing.

None of this had anything to do with how I felt in 1987 when Art Kaminsky revealed that Swanson's plan to get rid of me involved taking over Howard Cosell's chair on boxing telecasts. I had a contract at ABC Sports that ran for at least a few more years. Swanson wanted me to walk away from that contract, and one clear signal of that was his intention to assign me to a sport that didn't have a future in commercial TV. So exactly what was I going to do about that?

————

In 1987 boxing more than any other visible sport in America was sampling new forms of television exposure, and the major premium pay-cable networks, HBO and Showtime, were already into it. Boxing became increasingly less attractive to commercial networks—irregular schedules, rights acquired one event at a time rather than in package deals, owned by colorful promoters rather than spectacularly successful mainstream businessmen—but was no problem for the two cable monoliths. And as individual franchises, rather than teams, the fighters were like movie stars and could be promoted and presented to the public in many of the same ways.

It was only a matter of weeks after I walked out of ABC that Kaminsky reported the first boxing outreach. Showtime was doing a boxing card in St. Tropez, the famous French beach resort, and they wanted me to call the blow by blow. It was pitched as a one-time-only trial run—and a paid trip to a famous place I had never seen.

It was a doubleheader in the cruiserweight class: Evander Holyfield vs. Ossie Ocasio and Lee Roy Murphy vs. Dwight Muhammad Qawi. We were fewer than three minutes into the broadcast when the first pair of bare breasts appeared, a French Riviera opportunity that no commercial network could or would have employed at the time.

That happened often enough in the broadcast. I later adopted a stock descriptive line: "It was indisputably the most beautiful boxing telecast ever."

Whatever it was, it did the trick. Even before my departure from ABC, Mike Tyson had moved on to be the boxing centerpiece at HBO, which had broadcast Ray Leonard vs. Tommy Hearns and later Leonard vs. Marvin Hagler. I was grateful to Showtime for its interest, but I made it clear to Kaminsky that I wanted to call fights only for HBO.

I had no real reason to think that would happen. HBO's fights had been ably called for years by an outstanding broadcaster, Barry Tompkins, and I was a fan of his work. But I also knew that as a longtime ABC Sports entity, I occupied a higher rung on the ladder than Barry had reached. It seemed reasonable enough that if executives at HBO were looking to upgrade, I would be the logical choice. And I was developing a dialogue with Ross Greenburg, executive producer of their telecasts.

Not long after the trip to St. Tropez, Art called to say that Ross's superiors, sports division president Seth Abraham and board chairman Michael Fuchs, were planning to be in Los Angeles and wanted to meet me. Art was quite specific in saying, "This will be the most important meeting you can take. HBO is not a corporate beehive like the commercial networks. Authority is tightly held by small groups of people. Seth reports to Michael, and Michael reports to nobody. So be at your best and it is a great opportunity."

I couldn't have been more in agreement. I bought into their promotional mantra: "It's not TV. It's HBO." And as the voice of early Tyson fights at ABC, I felt the guiding hand of the universe at my back.

The meeting took place after my early evening KCBS-TV News shows at a chic hotel, maybe the Beverly Hills Hotel. It is now more a blur than it should be just because I was so in awe of HBO.

I had met Seth, so he greeted me in the lobby and took me to Michael's private bungalow. The three of us sat down in the living room. The first 15 minutes were devoted to how much they loved and respected Barry Tompkins and that no information leaks take place before they could tell him personally, and how I was never at liberty to say anything critical or demeaning about him.

Not that I would have, anyway, but I was impressed. The contrast between HBO's culture and that of the new Arledge-free ABC Sports was graphic. Kaminsky had told me, "Be positive but be cool. Don't fall all over yourself in gratitude for emerging on top."

I did the best I could with that, but my heart was beating fast. I had lost my chair on ABC's Saturday afternoon boxing telecasts, which were sliding toward irrelevance, and I was getting the story of Mike Tyson back. They were negotiating an extended deal for his rights. Talk about smelling like a rose!

They made it clear the deal would be lucrative. They were a top-shelf network with top-shelf talent commanding top-shelf fees, so Kaminsky would be pleased with whatever deal he made for me. And silently I was totaling up the numbers—KCBS-TV, CBS Sports, WFAN Radio, now HBO. It was mind-boggling. Thank you, Dennis Swanson! Irony upon irony.

When I got back to my suite at the Mondrian, the phone rang, and it was Art. He had already spoken to Seth. "Are you happy? They love you and they are very excited.

"You didn't even talk about Wimbledon with them and that might be your favorite part of the deal, given that Joanne and your daughters now live in London."

He was right, we hadn't even discussed it. But, yes, that was the icing on the cake, at least for now. I was still hoping to patch things up with Joanne and reunite with Brooke and Victoria, but it seemed like a long shot. Being their neighbor for three weeks every summer would be a consolation prize. And the status of the fights on HBO would give me a platform to become the number one blow-by-blow commentator in boxing.

I was still in the first year following my brutal excommunication from ABC, and Bree Walker had yet to enter the picture.

Before Mike Tyson and I left ABC Sports behind, I had called Tyson's spectacular blowouts of Jesse Ferguson and Marvis Frazier. Because of that, a fair portion of the general sports audience overlooked that Mike's 10-round decision over James "Quick" Tillis was not a knockout, and in the eyes of some veteran observers, it had exposed some flaws in Tyson's game. But the mystique remained in place.

When Tyson fought New Yorker Mitch "Blood" Green in May 1986, the bout was far from a continuation of their loud shouting match and near-violent encounter at a popular Harlem clothing store, with Tyson winning a 10-round decision and Green holding on for dear life at the final bell.

Kaminsky reported the following week that no upward momentum had been generated with Swanson, but there was more than three and a half years left on the existing contract Roone Arledge had given me and Swanson was trying to tear up.

I hadn't encountered that before in the inner world of network politics, but I was getting it now. If the division president just didn't like me, he just didn't like me. End of story. But we weren't quite there yet.

By his next TV fight, Tyson was on HBO. Then in November, he got his first legit heavyweight title shot against World Boxing Council title-holder Trevor Berbick, and his second-round left hook floored Berbick three times. Mike became, at age 20, the youngest heavyweight champion in history. Barry Tompkins's call of the knockout was exciting, as it should have been, and I had every reason to believe I had worked my last Mike Tyson fight. HBO had options on him, and he was exactly the kind of one-and-only-one attraction that premium pay-cable television coveted.

But in the following year everything changed. Kaminsky talked me into agreeing to a no-fault divorce with ABC Sports. I quickly migrated to Los Angeles, KCBS-TV, and the general CBS universe. We retained a contract on the HBO boxing deal. Michael Fuchs and Seth Abraham decided to offload Barry Tompkins and bet on me.

And by March 1988 I was in Tokyo to cover the Mike Tyson vs. Tony Tubbs fight, Mike's last before his beloved manager, Jimmy Jacobs, died. His death, which came two days after the fight, left control to partner Bill

Cayton, whom Mike reportedly distrusted. Tyson's new wife, rising star actress Robin Givens, clearly had his ear, and her mother, Ruth Roper, clearly had her daughter's ear.

On fight night, it was fortunate for Tyson that in the ring and his corner, his ear still belonged to Cus D'Amato's surrogate Kevin Rooney. Tubbs arrived predictably overweight and undertrained, two traits that had become career signatures for him, and in the second round Tyson caught him with a perfect body shot followed by an uppercut. Tubbs went down and there was no need for a count.

The most prophetic line of the telecast was authored by the great Larry Merchant in a commentary on the Mike and Robin public drama before the opening bell.

"Throughout boxing history, heavyweight champions have married early and often, and seldom to their benefit."

The lightning-rod couple were divorced on Valentine's Day 1989, less than one year later. By that time Mike was also headed toward an eventual divorce with Kevin Rooney, a move most observers agreed was orchestrated by promoter Don King, who had a share of all Tyson's pay-per-view fights. And the question lingered: Who in the world could possibly beat Mike Tyson?

Eventually I learned another great Larry Merchant line: "Boxing is the theater of the unexpected."

20

Anchors Away

After being driven out of ABC Sports by a sworn career enemy in 1987, I had landed on my feet as sports director at KCBS-TV in Los Angeles with a contract to call NFL games and other events for the CBS network.

The process with CBS was predetermined and perfunctory. In early September 1987 I flew from JFK to LAX, rented a car, and drove to the Oakwood Gardens short-term apartment rental complex near Burbank up the hill from the Warner Bros. studios. My starkly institutional two-bedroom had an alluring view into Beachwood Canyon, with the iconic "Hollywood" sign at the top.

A couple of days later I turned in my rental car and bought a new Porsche 911, a luxury I never allowed myself on the chaotic streets of Manhattan but now seemed obligatory for the new sports director star of KCBS-TV. When I parked it in my personal space at the KCBS-TV lot on Sunset Boulevard, I felt smugly at home.

And I eagerly made the rounds of my beat, greeting all the key executives and coaches and stars of the Rams, the Dodgers, the Lakers, the Kings, USC, and UCLA as though they were old friends, a fiction in which they all indulged me because it was politically correct. Even my head-to-head competitors—Fred Roggin of KNBC-TV and Jim Hill, now of KABC-TV—greeted me warmly and welcomed me when I bumped into them. I recognized how hard they worked within the confines of their different styles: Roggin liked to stay in the studio and write what amounted in some ways to a brilliant comic take on sports events, while Hill worked tirelessly to know everyone and be everywhere. At our first sit-down meeting to discuss the editorial focus, KCBS news director Erik Sorenson said to me, "The most valuable approach you can take is to begin each day with an intelligent forecast of where Hill is going to be that day and to whom he will speak and go from there."

That made sense and it became the heart of my MO. There was no point in trying to duplicate what Roggin did on KNBC or what the even more obtuse (but talented) Keith Olbermann was doing at the independent station KTLA. That wasn't my style. I was a straightforward sports editorial thinker, like Hill, and I needed to compete directly with him on his turf. That required getting to know the stars and dealing with them face-to-face. Hill was way ahead of me in terms of established relationships. But LA was about stars, and I had a long background as a network guy doing network stuff, and on that I would now capitalize.

I began to build my daily contact list around the biggest names in LA sports: Pat Riley, Magic Johnson, Orel Hershiser, Jim Everett, John Robinson, James Worthy, Kirk Gibson, and various others who drove headlines day after day.

I made some peremptory efforts to find a house, and on a couple of occasions lured Joanne into bringing my daughters out from New York to search with me. After the first two months I got tired of the Oakwood Gardens and moved into a small suite at the Mondrian hotel on Sunset Boulevard, which had a better poolside crowd and was a more logical launching pad from which to explore the late-night parties in the canyons above Hollywood.

Joanne soon retained a divorce attorney in New York, and we began the gut-wrenching process of carving up all the windfall money I was now making. My first divorce from Linda had been easy and friendly, so I stupidly assumed this one would be that way, too. Eventually I saw how wrong I had been. I promised myself I would find ways to make up for the damage to my daughters. But now, 36 years later, that process continues, as it should.

I learned that a life obsessed entirely with work and money might leave me unbearably lonely, and few living spaces are more inhospitable to that emptiness than Hollywood. Sometimes, pointlessly, I fantasize about what I would do differently if I were now back in 1988. And the simplest answer might be "everything." But life is a take. There are no rehearsals. And whatever you do right now is what you are going to live with. Few people I have known would have been wise enough to turn down the opportunities I had.

I was still fresh in that transformation when the Dodgers won the National League pennant and entered the 1988 World Series against the heavily favored Oakland A's. As the sports correspondent for *CBS This Morning*, I was about to have an extraordinarily heavy workload until one of those teams won four games and simplified my life.

Meanwhile, after a handful of trips to Los Angeles with my daughters to visit and house hunt with me, Joanne had gone back to New York and sent me a final announcement: She wasn't coming. She had no desire to live in Los Angeles, it wasn't her fault I had wound up there, and 10 years together had been quite enough for her.

The better part of valor was to try to maintain friendship and hope to change her mind over time. I knew there might be obstacles. For reasons I wasn't sure about, she had disappeared to London for several weeks the summer before, when I was calling my last several scheduled events before leaving ABC. If my daughters weren't going to live in Los Angeles, it would be far better for me if they lived in New York, not London. I accepted the diplomatic reality, at least for now. A campaign to save the marriage was physically impossible if they weren't coming to Los Angeles.

My 13 colorful years at ABC had left me with a vast catalog of friendships in the sports world, and LA was the capital of that world.

Around Labor Day 1987 when I went to KCBS, I had been in the serious TV business since I was 24 and had never worked for a station. Now my primary occupation was to be a local sports director. I would be working for a living, appearing on at least three shows a day, commanding a staff that included a producer, an editor, and another on-air reporter. This was the step I had skipped on my way to college football and *Wide World of Sports* in the 13 years before.

Now a contractor with HBO in 1988, I went back to Wimbledon immediately after calling the Tyson-Spinks fight in Atlantic City that lasted 91 seconds, fully expecting to see a tournament victory by the knockout wunderkind of tennis, Germany's Boris Becker. At age 20 he had already won there twice, and it seemed obvious to me no other player benefited so much from the faster properties of the grass surface. He made it to the final but lost to the elegant Swede Stefan Edberg, by which time I was flying to New York to fulfill a mandate from Art Kaminsky with which I at first disagreed.

Art called to insist I change my travel plan back to Los Angeles in response to a CBS News request that I stop off in New York to co-host the Monday morning edition of the show that competed with *Today* on NBC and *Good Morning America* on ABC. Harry Smith was taking the day off—it was July 4—and his co-anchor, Kathleen Sullivan, had worked the late-night ABC segments from the Winter Olympics in Sarajevo with me four years before. Art said CBS wanted to see how we looked together.

It was the first time I pushed back against Art, who repeated what had become his favorite retort.

"Jim, you're only 38 years old. We're just getting started. When one door closes, another one opens."

He knew I had no interest in morning news, but he was right in general. Still, I was reluctant.

"Art, Monday is July 4. It's all barbecues and fireworks and no one will be watching."

"Laurence Tisch (chief executive officer of CBS) will be watching. Howard Stringer [president of the news division] will be watching. You will be speaking directly to them."

I changed my travel from Saturday London to LA to Sunday London to New York. The weather was clear that afternoon in the city as I checked into the Regency on Park Avenue and turned on the TV. Just because I would be sitting on a news set the following morning I searched for CNN. A surface-to-air missile fired from an American warship had shot down an Iran Air jetliner in the Persian Gulf, killing all 290 people aboard. This was a global story, and the show would no longer be all barbecue and fireworks.

A few hours later a production assistant banged on my door and dropped off a folder with the rundown and format for the show. My eyes popped. In the first segment after Kathleen covered the taped pictures from the Gulf, I interviewed the secretary of defense. In the next segment I debriefed the chairman of the Senate Armed Services Committee. Later I did five minutes with a widely published Middle East editorialist.

It was that way throughout the show. I even touched on news stories other than the errant destruction of the passenger jet. It was still a sunny July 4 day when my noon flight from JFK touched down at LAX. I went to the Mondrian in room 510 and crashed.

When I awoke, I had a message to call the concierge. She asked me to come pick up a written note, which I instantly recognized to be in the handwriting of my immediate boss, Erik Sorenson. I was being summoned to a 7 AM meeting in his news director office at KCBS-TV. Seven AM? Something highly unusual was up.

The newsroom was totally empty when I arrived at 6:55. Casually dressed, Erik quickly thanked me for making myself available at the odd hour, then established we wouldn't waste any time because he and his family were catching a plane later that morning for a vacation in Hawaii. He pointed to stacks and stacks of three-quarter-inch tapes in black plastic boxes that lined the wall below the panoramic glass window into the newsroom.

"You see all these tapes? Do you have any idea what they are?"

"No, not really. What are they?"

"That's every up-and-coming male local news anchor in the country. Dozens of them, coast to coast, every top 50 market. Do you know what we are doing with those tapes today?"

"I don't know." (I truly didn't.) "What are you doing with those tapes today?"

Erik had prominent dancing eyebrows that rose precipitously, Jack Nicholson–style, toward the top of his forehead when he was excited. He was in full "all work and no play makes Johnny a dull boy" form as he prepared for the punch line.

Fairly shouting now, as there was no one there to hear him: "We're throwing them into the dumpster back at the barrier of the parking lot by El Centro. Do you know why?"

Playing along, because I wasn't hip yet. "No Erik, I don't know why. Why?"

"BECAUSE WE FOUND OUR NEWS ANCHOR! He showed up on the network morning news set yesterday in New York! We're going to rebuild this operation around you."

The work was deceptively difficult in that I had little experience writing my own copy. I was coming along, and really liked my co-anchor, a grounded LA veteran named Tritia Toyota. She was well known, and I figured she could be a friend and ally for years to come.

We were in our third week together doing the 5 and 11 shows when one day as we were watching a taped story, she slid my copy page over toward her on the desk and scribbled on it: "You are about to have a new co-anchor."

I shot her an incredulous look and wrote, "Who?"

She pulled it back and scrawled, "Brie Walker." I later learned that was a misspelling. The name was "Bree."

My turn again. "Who is that?"

Talking during tape on the set was generally frowned upon unless it was totally necessary. Tritia knew that far better than I did.

She threw her head back and literally shouted. "You don't know? My God, what a yokel you are. You don't know? She's the hottest local anchor in the country."

I didn't know. Bree Walker was at that moment on the air at WCBS-TV in New York. Within a few days I would learn a lot. She had gone to New York a year or so before from San Diego after having had her choice of network owned-and-operated stations in a full-scale bidding war. She had been treated to that after achieving focus research scores for recognizability and likability that were among the highest ever seen in the industry. And having been born with a congenital hand and foot anomaly called ectrodactyly, she was possibly the most celebrated person in the culture with a visible physical difference. She was a walking feature story, a legend in the making. And now, for reasons not clear or not articulated, she wanted out of New York.

Later in the week of the Tritia Toyota on-set discussion, Erik Sorenson pulled me into his office and sat me down in front of a monitor.

"Here, I am going to give you a look to settle your curiosity. Then I am going to shut this off because I don't want you to draw premature conclusions. And she was pregnant at the time this was shot, but her little girl was born in August. So watch."

He rolled the tape. Truly platinum hair, sleek. Coal-black eyes that jumped through the lens. A calm, measured, resonant voice. A glimpse of the hands, different but not the dominant image. An easy smile, and just as easily a transition back to the serious anchor mode. She was sensational. She was SCARY good. Erik switched off the monitor.

I went back to my desk. This could be very good. Or it could be bad. Was I going to be that good? For the first time I began to wonder.

In October, after the Dodgers won the World Series, I now had no official role in the station's sports coverage but was still the sports correspondent for *CBS This Morning*. In that capacity I spent the whole night in the company of manager Tom Lasorda, seeking a guarantee that he would appear on our network in the morning (he did) and to prevent him from showing up on *Today* or *Good Morning America* (he didn't).

I was mildly hung over and totally without sleep when I rolled my new Porsche over the ridge to participate in a KCBS-TV welcome lunch on Ventura Boulevard for Bree Walker. She and her husband and daughter had arrived from New York, and along with Erik Sorenson, station manager Bob Hyland, and a few others from the newsroom staff, I was there to make her feel at home. It was illuminating.

My first impression was that she was prim, civilized, and well-mannered in a way that would need me to be careful. She was originally from Minnesota, and her father had run a gas station. Middle American. Her husband and daughter were going to the hotel, so I offered Bree a ride back to the station.

When we all left to follow the executives back to KCBS-TV, Bree reached for the volume knob to crank up U2's *Rattle and Hum* disc in my stereo. NO ONE, certainly no woman in conservative business attire, ever turned up my volume. Quite the opposite. But she cranked it and flashed me a devilish grin, and just like that it was on. Looking back, I would have to say we were in heat by the time we reached the station at 6121 Sunset. Fifteen minutes at most.

Later I would reflect that Sorenson, in discussing the politics of the newsroom and the pressures that would surround a brand-new primary anchor team, had at one point said to me, "The two of you will need to be joined at the hip." And we both knew how to follow orders.

From the first get-acquainted lunch with management, we were falling hopelessly in love. It began as an uncontrollable obsession and eventually added an element of defense mechanism. She had made clear from the first day that her marriage to Robert Walker was on the rocks. I could see from the mounting evidence that my marriage to Joanne Mallis was over, and I was relieved by that. Joanne brought our daughters to visit me, but we had given up living in LA together.

As 1989 moved toward 1990, I was still in the Mondrian hotel, and Bree and I were working with lawyers to bring an end—as quietly as possible—to our now-forsaken attachments. Station management knew, because the intensity of it all was impossible for us to hide. Every one of our colleagues in the newsroom knew, because newsrooms are only slightly less intimate than bedrooms. Every other meaningful news professional in the Los Angeles market knew, because two people can keep a secret only if one of the two is dead. And little more than two scant years after the whole experiment had begun, speculation was rampant at KABC-TV and KNBC-TV as to which prominent Channel Two news anchor, Jim or Bree, would be first canceled from the 5 and 11 news due mainly to all the rumors flying.

The ratings were up, but only marginally. And sometimes the male anchor looked so woefully deflated in the two-shot. I looked like an eagle who had gotten his wings clipped while reading the script on camera. Only in free-streaming situations, like election nights, or spontaneous break-ins, like earthquakes or car chases, was I genuinely at home as a news anchor.

Being overshadowed by my own wife made that period painful. Under tacit pressure from KCBS-TV, we got married in 1990, starring publicly in a glorious wedding ceremony on the cliff overlooking the Pacific behind the Ritz-Carlton, Laguna Niguel. News helicopters from all the major LA stations circled for camera shots in the sky. Bree's infant daughter, Andrea Walker, was a flower girl. My two daughters stayed in New York with Joanne.

And now we were legitimized, which might have been logically expected to remove some of the pressures we had created for ourselves. But really, no such luck. Whether we were covering unprecedented Chinese student protests in Tiananmen Square, or the First Gulf War, or the police beating of Rodney King, or any of the other major stories that entered the newsroom in 1990 and 1991, it almost always felt to me like Bree was assigned to read the lead, the first appearance on camera in the show.

But real or not, my pathetically crestfallen responses were affecting everything, from relations with colleagues in the newsroom to relations between newly minted anchor-husband and anchor-wife in our newly purchased home near Lake Hollywood, right up the hill from Axl Rose and down the street from Queen Latifah.

Given my status and the numbers in my contract, it just didn't seem possible that these things could affect my position. The station needed Bree, after all, and Bree needed and wanted me, so we'd be given the time to work it out. But local news is all about ratings, and despite Bree's powerful presence, the ratings were stalled. So despite all my rationalizations, Armageddon was coming.

Bree was less than thrilled. "I can see what is happening here. You are going back to sports television, all the travel, all the glamour, all the national exposure without the encumbrance of the day-to-day and the newsroom. The shoulder-to-shoulder teamwork we had envisioned in this marriage is going away. You will be out at night in clubs and restaurants, and all the women who chased you before will be back in your life."

It was a natural fear, given what was perceived to have happened to our previous marriages. I assured her it was neither the purpose nor the intended outcome. Our marriage was the special one, and anything that happened back out on the road would strictly be about work. But privately, was I happy to get away from the newsroom?

Sure, and in no small measure happy to get away from being outperformed nightly by my own wife on the air.

21

Tokyo Takedown

Preparing for the next big fight (Courtesy of Jeff Julian)

A s the late-night host and the swimming stroke-by-stroke commentator at the 1984 Olympics in Los Angeles, I applauded the stirring success turned in by the American boxing team. I wondered what this bumper crop of gold medalists—nine of them—might mean to future assignments at ABC. But bridging from 1986 into 1987, I wound up doing blow by blow on telecasts involving most of them. And that became part of my portfolio walking in the door of HBO in 1988.

It was striking even to this day that Mike Tyson did not make that Olympic team, losing in the heavyweight final at the Olympic trials to Henry Tillman. When they faced each other again as professionals in 1990, Tyson kayoed Tillman in the first round, reminding the public of his dramatic demolitions of outmatched opponents. Lesser performances against trickier styles were quickly forgotten or overlooked.

Meanwhile, his Olympic teammates were building profiles. I had already called blow by blow on ABC telecasts of gold medalists Meldrick Taylor, Pernell Whitaker, and Mark Breland. Now I awaited their graduation to HBO.

I became more conscious of storytelling advantages in commercial-free boxing. For decades on network television, the convenient convergence of the one-minute commercial and the one-minute break in the corner had buttressed business but robbed fans of critical elements of the narrative. On HBO (and Showtime) the between-rounds minute became a treasure trove of material: interplays between fighters and their trainers, the race against time to treat and inhibit bleeding and swelling, an occasional visit from the referee. All that was needed to tell those stories and let our cameras and microphones do their work.

As time went by, that effective naturalism began to bleed into my work in other ways.

Even during rounds, I was learning that less is always more. If the audience could hear the thoughts and observations of Sugar Ray Leonard and Larry Merchant, the better I was as the blow-by-blow voice.

That increasing team comfort coalesced beautifully in what became the groundbreaking telecast for that period in boxing and my own HBO arc.

After Tyson demolished Michael Spinks in 91 seconds on June 27, 1988, his next fight was eight months later, February 25, 1989, against Frank Bruno in Las Vegas. He was less than perfect and got jolted by a left hook in the first round but easily recovered en route to a fifth-round TKO.

Five months after that, he was back in ferocious form at Atlantic City, taking all of 93 seconds to waste Carl Williams with glancing blows. It seemed like there was no end in sight for the Tyson dynasty. With Spinks already behind him and a sparse division in front of him, he appeared ready to write a lengthy heavyweight chapter. The best opponent Don King could find for Mike was Buster Douglas, a known underachiever who had lost to Tony Tucker and beaten Oliver McCall. Those were not flashy credentials.

I confess to buying into the consensus that Tyson-Douglas was one of the most egregious mismatches in recent heavyweight history; on the other hand, I did see things two days before the fight that suggested strange possibilities. Tyson was in shape but clearly depressed by difficulties in his marital life and focused more on a morbid documentary film titled *Faces of Death* than on the opponent. His camp underlings revealed he had watched it dozens of times. And Douglas was busy making friends and signing autographs, accepting polite encouragement from the Tyson-obsessed locals. Those things were visible.

In the years since, I've come to the conclusion Tyson should never have been a 42–1 favorite in the fight. There was considerable evidence to the contrary, starting with James "Quick" Tillis and continuing through James "Bonecrusher" Smith, José Ribalta, and his turn with Tony Tucker. It would be difficult for Mike to dominate opponents who were taller, could move, and had a jab. At six feet four, Douglas had basketball training in his background and a long jab with some pop. And he could bring the right hand over the top where the shorter Tyson would have trouble seeing it coming.

And that paragraph describes most of the fight. Ray Leonard, Larry Merchant, and I were incredulous, but by the third round we knew what we were watching. And in an American setting we would have been generating a lot of excitement building toward one of the biggest upsets in sports history, but in Tokyo's Dome on the morning of February 11, 1990, before roughly 34,000 spectators, we were talking softly, as though we were calling figure skating or golf, because the crowd was almost silent. You could hear the leather soles of Buster and Mike's shoes slapping against the canvas—that's how quiet it was. So the three of us sat there whispering, adding understated captions to boxing's single most arresting moment of the pay-cable television era, and we flew home in a daze.

In the late rounds of Tyson-Douglas I thought, *Wow, the very first live prizefight you ever attended, Cassius Clay vs. Sonny Liston, was instantly identified in the media as the biggest upset in boxing history. Now you are doing live blow by blow on the fight that will replace it in terms of that identity.*

And Monday morning one national newspaper TV critic called it "one of the greatest telecasts ever in sports TV because Lampley and Leonard and Merchant had been so devoted to sitting back and letting the story tell itself." Little did he know it was all an accident, an unanticipated response to an unanticipated condition that we just couldn't have planned for the undefeated heavyweight champion.

———

By early December 1991 CBS had seen enough to know what it wanted to do. Bob Hyland, the general manager of KCBS-TV, summoned me to his office. When I notified Art Kaminsky, he instantly had a hunch what they had in mind and said to listen and not to say yes to anything. Art pointed out, "You still have three deals: one to anchor news for the station, another to be the sports correspondent for the network morning show, and a third to narrate NFL football games on Sundays in the fall. Each arrangement is separate from the others, so they can't just collapse them all without paying you three ways."

So the forecast was cloudy, but it wasn't raining quite yet. I went to Hyland's office and sat across the desk from him. CBS News chieftain Eric Ober joined us from New York via telephone speaker. The mood was friendly but resigned.

The news ratings had not risen, and the division wasn't seeing enough of the Jim and Bree shows to establish acceptable growth. The audience still liked and respected me, but in comparison to Bree, they did not see me as an everyday news enhancement. This wasn't a statement on my performance or my aptitude, audiences are fickle, and in some ways it was a compliment—most viewers, particularly men, still saw me as a major sports presence and didn't understand why I was anchoring news. They suspected it might be because Bree and I were making some of the news instead of covering it.

To the contrary, the network had a wonderful opportunity for me. Coming in another month, CBS Sports was the American provider for the Winter Olympics in Albertville, France. All the network assignments were set up, but these new circumstances pointed the way to a great idea. If I agreed to go straight from my news anchor desk to Albertville a few days before the opening ceremony and begin providing daily and nightly news and feature stories to all the CBS affiliate stations, I would have a high-profile assignment to momentarily redefine me while someone else (they didn't yet know who) moved into the chair next to Bree at 5 and 11 in LA. And when I came back from France I would go back to being the sports director. They asserted the existing contract gave them the right to mandate that.

I went back to my office and called Art, who was in no way surprised and said it could have been worse; and it was pure fiction that they could simply reassign me as the local sports director. The contract gave them no such right. If I just walked away from CBS and erased the stigma of a demotion, I had the legal right to do that. The trick was finding an alternative perch to equal the status I was leaving. In the meantime, I should go to Albertville, perform the storytelling task they wanted, and do it as well as I could amid unfortunate emotional turmoil. As small consolation, I would be adding another Olympics assignment, my sixth, to the five I had gathered at ABC Sports.

And what I did best, clearer than ever, was boxing on HBO. Live, no commercials, narrative storytelling in a personality-dwarfed sport where I began and ended almost every on-air paragraph. Increasingly, that was becoming my signature.

I arrived in Albertville a few days before the opening ceremony. CBS had not been to the Olympics for quite a while due to Roone Arledge's obsession to keep the games at ABC Sports. The broadcast center had some new names, including the creatively chosen host team of baseball expert commentator Tim McCarver and newswoman Paula Zahn. With every day came new faces to recognize and familiar ones to reidentify. On the second day, in a narrow hallway outside the research office, I surprisingly bumped into Dick Ebersol, the first network executive to have interviewed me in the ABC college-age reporter search nearly 18 years before.

The shock was amplified by my instant recollection that Dick didn't work for CBS. He had left Arledge and ABC in 1974 to become head of late-night weekend programming at NBC, where he helped NBC producer Lorne Michaels create the weekly phenomenon *Saturday Night Live*.

As we shook hands I remembered he now was president of NBC

Sports. So after being groomed by Roone, and then splitting from ABC to fly with his own wings, Ebersol had what amounted to his mentor's position at a competing network. But why was he at the CBS Olympics facility in the snowy French Alps?

"Oh, my gosh, Jim Lampley! I had heard you might be here, and I'm so glad I found you. We have something to talk about."

"We do? Very interesting. What's on your mind?"

"Well, to be honest, most likely we don't, because I know how well you are doing in LA. But it's too bad, because if you weren't so on fire at KCBS I would present you with an offer here and now."

"What offer?"

"I need a late-night anchor at Barcelona this summer. And you are the best man in the world for the job."

"Well, I should probably tell you just to call Art. But since I don't know how long it might take for you to reach him, I'll go ahead and give away the punch line. Dick, I just got fired at KCBS. I'm free as a wild hawk for Barcelona. Do you want Art Kaminsky's number?"

"I've got it. I'll reach out tonight. Start making plans to be in Spain this summer. This is my wildest dream."

"Mine, too."

And just like that, I was about to add another network to my resume and with it my seventh Olympics assignment.

NBC executive producer Terry O'Neil, a deeply trusted former ABC colleague with whom I had a long history of work and friendship experiences, made it clear to me that my arrival could lead to bigger prominence than I had ever enjoyed. I would co-host the late-night segments at Barcelona with Hannah Storm. I would cover NFL games in the fall with my friend Ahmad Rashad.

Eventually, I would be installed as host of golf and studio host of the NFL, and my calendar filled with fun, with meaningful assignments from

Ebersol and O'Neil. I celebrated by taking my daughter Brooke to Barcelona as my guest and companion for the Olympics, the seventh of an eventual 14 for four networks.

Bree was stuck in the news anchor chair at KCBS-TV in Los Angeles and seething with envy. But what could she say? This was what I had done to build my career before the fateful accident that made me a news anchor and introduced me to her life. CBS had made network-level decisions to build the identity and financial fortunes of its most valuable owned-and-operated station, KCBS-TV, around us as a news anchor team. It took about two years for us, mostly me, to throw all that into tabloid-style chaos. We brought massive damage to my career, but I still had my sportscaster identity and my HBO contract to fall back on. We did greater and more irreparable harm to Bree's career, and it would take decades for us to sort out and accommodate the emotional fallout from that.

22

The Reckoning

By 1992 I was no longer anchoring newscasts with Bree Walker at KCBS-TV in Los Angeles, and I had signed a contract with NBC Sports that sent me to Barcelona to be the late-night co-host—with Hannah Storm—at the Summer Olympics.

There was an astonishing story convergence awaiting me there on two fronts: the Dream Team, the first participation of professional players in the Olympic basketball competition, included Magic Johnson, who had become a helpful friend and news source during the time I worked the Lakers beat; and a 19-year-old East Los Angeles boxer was by far the reigning attraction in that competition, seeking to win the gold medal in honor of his beloved and recently deceased mother. His name, almost musical in its beauty, was Oscar De La Hoya.

After De La Hoya won his Barcelona gold, I was quite sure I would see him again in another network setting and yes, shortly after returning to Los Angeles, he signed an entry-platform contract with HBO that made him a centerpiece of the boxing franchise for years thereafter.

I called a lengthy string of Oscar's fights, including two victories over

Mexican all-time great Julio César Chávez, his controversial decision over Pernell Whitaker, his even more debatable loss to Félix Trinidad, his two decision defeats to boyhood rival and friend Shane Mosley, his vengeful victory over Fernando Vargas, and his largely pointless exercises (at least for him) versus Bernard Hopkins, Floyd Mayweather, and Manny Pacquiao. Oscar lost fights, but he never lost his audience because he always competed with visible passion and pride. That is the nature of boxing for upper-level competitors; your wins are more numerous than your losses; the most rabid viewers will internalize the painful nights. Oscar finished with 39 wins, 30 of them by knockout, six losses, and countless memories and thrills.

What De La Hoya did for my career and for HBO boxing in general is incalculable. Among other things, when HBO management had a falling-out in the early '90s with Sugar Ray Leonard, Oscar's presence on our network helped attract George Foreman to work with Larry Merchant and me as our expert commentator.

Ray had a self-admitted obstacle to saying goodbye to his fighting career. After his disputed decision win over Marvin Hagler for the middleweight championship, he had kept looking for paychecks that satisfied his financial hunger and for matchups that stirred his competitive fire. The Hagler fight was on April 6, 1987. Leonard announced his retirement on May 27. He announced his comeback in July 1988, and on November 7 I called his catchweight fight against light heavyweight champion Donny Lalonde. Ray was hurt early in the fight by the larger Lalonde, but he rallied in the ninth round to score a TKO win and become the super middleweight champion.

That set up another fight I called on HBO, the long-awaited rematch with Roberto Duran. The aging Panamanian star was listless, and so was the fight. Ray won by an easy unanimous decision, and the Las Vegas crowd booed. Ray had been cut several times by head butts and was given 60 stitches.

So, enough? No. Ray was now offered a fight on Showtime against 154-pound champion Terry Norris. This time HBO was not invited to bid for the telecast rights, and by going ahead with the fight Ray prompted HBO management to seek a replacement for the expert commentator chair next to me.

And while all this had been going on, one of the most popular personalities in the sport, former heavyweight champion George Foreman, was reconstructing his boxing career. At the same time, he was creating a wildly effective persona as a smiling pitchman for hamburger grills, automobile mufflers, big man's clothing, and various other successful ventures. All he had to do to sell products was to flash his massive and beguiling smile.

We had begun showing some of his fights, and we knew from meetings with him that he was interesting and persuasive when talking about ring strategy and tactics. And he was respectful of Larry for his integrity and all his years of covering the sport.

Foreman loved star power, so his favorite fighter at that moment was Oscar De La Hoya.

With all that going for us, HBO management had made a deal with George to succeed Ray Leonard as HBO Sports ringside boxing expert.

I had no idea what Big George thought about me. It wasn't clear. But we would see, and I imagined it would be fun. But fun is only one part of the interplay between a blow-by-blow voice and an expert commentator. Ray Leonard was recognized universally as a master stylist and tactician, while George was mostly recognized as a puncher, a master blaster. Could he illuminate a featherweight fight? We were about to find out.

That would be the least of our worries. Not only did George offer meaningful opinions about every kind of fight and every kind of fighter, those opinions were also strong enough that if he disagreed with something Larry or I said on the air, he instantly stepped forward to say so.

Viewers made it clear in comments on the internet that they assumed any editorial disagreement during fight calls was uncomfortable for us and the network. That might have been true if someone was insecure enough to feel isolated by that. And if one of us was most susceptible to that it was probably me, just because George and Larry had seen more prize fights. But we all understood a little roughhousing among the talking dogs was probably good for subscription sales. And I don't recall a single time Seth Abraham or Ross Greenburg ever said, "Hey, be careful about getting into disagreements with Larry and George." That just wasn't a concern. So as the '90s rolled forward and the fights played out, we became increasingly rambunctious.

A perfect example was the second fight between De La Hoya and his former amateur traveling partner Shane Mosley in Las Vegas on September 13, 2003. They had first met in Los Angeles in June 2000, a rousing battle that mixed tactical boxing brilliance with corresponding periods of toe-to-toe slugging and produced a widely accepted split decision in Mosley's favor. The negotiation for the rematch was difficult because, loss or no loss, Oscar was still the bigger star and therefore the bigger draw, while Shane wanted a deal that acknowledged he had won the first fight. Eventually the dispute was settled via an agreement that Mosley would earn a half-million-dollar bonus to be carved out of De La Hoya's share if he won again.

A constant bone of contention in our editorial flow was how much weight to delegate to CompuBox numbers, the still-nascent process of counting punches and differentiating between jabs and power that was gaining currency with some fans but faced an uphill fight with others. Larry was more skeptical than I was. George was somewhere in the middle.

On this night Oscar had a clear statistical edge, 221 total landed punches to 127 over the course of the 12 rounds. He had also thrown 120 more punches than Mosley. In most previous instances this would have computed to a clear De La Hoya decision, which was what Foreman and I expected to hear. But the ringside press corps was considerably less enthusiastic about CompuBox, and it turned out a large nucleus among the press perceived that Mosley had landed punches with more authority down the stretch of the fight. The judges agreed with them, and Mosley won a unanimous decision, 115–113 (seven rounds to five) on all three scorecards.

HBO unofficial ringside scorer Harold Lederman, who unlike his official ringside colleagues was privy throughout the fight to CompuBox numbers, had it 115–113 for De La Hoya. I pointed out that an instant poll of ringside sportswriters indicated staunch support for the official decision. Foreman suggested the decision was tainted by prejudice against De La Hoya's promoter, Bob Arum, and called for an investigation. Merchant was by now in the ring for the post-fight interviews, where Oscar's trainer for that fight, Floyd Mayweather Sr., declared the judges were "blind and senile."

Whether it was a perfect decision or a highway robbery, it was entertaining and reflective of the confounding subjectivity of boxing scoring. And looking back, it was a useful touchstone for understanding our telecast during the years George sat between Larry and me. He absolutely had expertise that included understanding the craft for fighters in all weight classes, even flyweights. I should not have doubted that. And while he was watching and describing other fights and fighters, he was in his own mind plotting and conjuring one more Big George moment, one that became the source of the title for this book. But we weren't there quite yet.

———

In 1992 Hannah Storm was the walking epitome of a woman network sportscaster in the United States. She had grown up in men's sports arenas, daughter of one of the most effective professional sports executives of that era, Mike Storen of the Indiana Pacers and Atlanta Hawks. She had enjoyed several productive years at CNN and Turner Sports before being recruited by NBC, and ultimately the network reached out to bring over the fellow sportscaster she had met and eventually married in Atlanta, Dan Hicks.

If you were looking at the hierarchy you might have concluded Hannah was just a bit higher on the NBC totem pole than Dan, but they never portrayed even a hint of friction. If Bree and I had allowed strong chemistry and dynamic market appeal to fatally contaminate our on-air romance, and I couldn't deny we had, Hannah and Dan were serenely above that. They were admirable in every way. Hannah was an impressively skilled professional and an effective partner with me on the late-night show.

She was also playful, which encouraged my own playful instincts, and together we persuaded show producer John McGuinness to title our on-air segments Club Barcelona, with a long Spanish U. In effect, Kloob Barcelona. It was inescapably that kind of town, and we were encouraged by Ebersol and Terry O'Neil to reach for non-sports subjects where appropriate, to try to broaden the 11:30 PM to 1 AM. East Coast audience, and maybe steal some viewers from CBS star David Letterman.

At 12, Brooke Lampley was old enough to leave the hotel or the broadcast center when appropriately accompanied to attend an event but young enough that I only felt secure if we began and ended every day and night together. So she spent a large amount of her time sitting on the back row in the control room, absorbing the games through our filter and occasionally offering a perspective only she could provide.

The overwhelming American sports focus of those games was on the first-ever participation by NBA players in Olympic competition. The US roster was stocked with living legends Michael Jordan, Magic Johnson, Larry Bird, Scottie Pippen, Charles Barkley, and Karl Malone, an

American delegation dubbed "the Dream Team." Its expected gold medal coronation would help erase the memory of the United States' controversial last-possession loss to the Soviet Union at the 1988 Olympics in Seoul, the first time the United States hadn't reached the gold medal game.

The manifest destiny of the Dream Team was omnipresent in the daily flourishes that kept viewers glued to the NBC coverage, and athletes from every sport and from nations around the globe acknowledged that they were just as enthralled as the public at large. The sheer glamour of the Olympics was dramatically multiplied for those two weeks in Barcelona.

Although Jordan was a Carolina icon, and I had interviewed him after he scored 63 points against the Celtics in the 1986 NBA playoffs, he (and Magic and Bird, etc.) gave most allotted TV media minutes to Bob Costas, who was hosting the prime-time slot. I did get a sit-down with Malone and found him to be kinder than his rugged reputation on the court.

Early in the first week, the on-air promotions office sent a note to producer John McGuinness suggesting a late-night show interview with a young actor who would be starring in a new CBS comedy series that fall. Unfamiliar with the name, McGuinness turned around in the control room and asked the dozen or so sports TV personnel assembled, "Hey, should we be interviewing someone named Will Smith here?"

There were several seconds of silence before Brooke piped up from the back row. "Yes, you definitely want to interview Will Smith."

Laughter, an embarrassed shrug from the only 12-year-old in the broadcast center, but at the end of the day McGuinness was no fool. Hannah sat down and taped with Will Smith later that day, and we were heroes with the network brass. And as the story circulated in the building, Hannah and Dan began promoting the nickname they had chosen for my daughter: the Dream Kid. It stuck, and I couldn't have said it better myself.

It was a mark of the late-night show's success that David Letterman chose, during the second week, to aggressively lampoon "Club Barcelona," making sure with snide dismissal to exaggerate the "kloob" pronunciation. Hannah and I had wondered aloud on the set whether we might have pushed that gambit too far, but when Letterman spoke up and poked fun, we knew we had touched a nerve. And as the closing weekend arrived, a soon-to-be-significant chapter began unfolding in my life, when a charismatic young American boxer, Oscar De La Hoya, arrived on the set to celebrate the gold medal he had emotionally won in tribute to his recently deceased mother.

At the Barcelona opening ceremony, I had carefully pointed out to Brooke how graphically we were seeing an old world passing and a new, more promising version walking in. For the first time, Black South Africans marched as equals alongside their white countrymen. For the last time, the Soviet Union competed as an aggregation, but now under the concocted banner of the Commonwealth of Independent States, they headed toward a future as separate individual republics, bearing the identities that had for 70 years been suppressed by tyranny. An archer fired a single arrow across a vast space to light the flame of this spirited new world, striking the target. It seemed, for that shining moment, that all good things were possible.

And never had I felt more optimistic about my career, looking ahead to the football season with Ahmad and the golf and NFL studio appearances to follow. But the challenging personal circumstances that had unraveled my news anchoring stint were still in place. Bree and I weren't yet back in a state of bliss as she adjusted to my frequent travels and local news ratings that still refused to budge. And circumstances surrounding us that neither of us controlled were conspiring to create more bumps in the road ahead.

First, it became clear that juggling HBO and NBC was challenging. Several times in the fall of 1992 I had NFL games to cover in one location Sunday following HBO boxing shows in a different location the prior Saturday night. I didn't miss a kickoff, the planes all stayed on time, but my preparation suffered and along with it the quality and status of the games to which Ahmad and I were assigned.

Then soon after that, O'Neil was removed as executive producer. He was surely my strongest advocate at NBC, but he had a history of head-strong turbulence—NBC was his third commercial network, and he had been fired from ABC and CBS due to friction with management. There was no shock in seeing it happen again, but it removed a layer of support. And there was poignancy in it for me. When producers at ABC Sports had begun two decades earlier to dream up the job of the college-age re-porter, the once-in-a-lifetime job that had given me a network television career, many insiders there viewed the whole process as a vehicle for get-ting O'Neil on the air. As you may remember, he had been the Olympics researcher at Munich in 1972 and a game-changing hero. At a time when even Soviet Olympics authorities had only the skimpiest information on gymnast Olga Korbut, the breakout star of those games, Terry interviewed her and had a full-page profile for Jim McKay and his colleagues.

But Terry didn't get the college reporter chance. I did. Despite that, he had been a sweet and loyal friend. And now, after another abrupt re-versal in his once-promising production career, he was out of network TV sports. A golf telecast producer named Tommy Roy, a far more skilled diplomat than Terry, was now the executive producer. I hadn't yet hosted my first golf tournament, and I had no idea what that would mean for me.

It got worse. When the time came for me to make my 1993 golf debut, at the glamorous Bob Hope Classic in the California desert, I had a sched-uling conflict due to a boxing match in Las Vegas. By the time I signed the NBC contract, I had made HBO my first priority. NBC had to accept the embarrassment of asking veteran broadcaster Charlie Jones, who had been dislodged from the job, to come back and sit in the 18th-hole tower again that weekend. Dick Ebersol made clear he wasn't happy about that.

That fall I hosted NFL coverage in the studio, working with Mike

Ditka, O.J. Simpson, and Will McDonough. Having hosted the ABC college football operation for six years in the 1980s, and due to the smaller number of teams and games, I found the NFL studio job technically easier. As a group we all got along well, and my 15-year acquaintanceship with O.J. was deepening. Most weekends we flew together between Los Angeles and New York. But five times during that season I had to call HBO fights on Saturday night and then fly overnight to New York to enter the studio functionally without sleep.

In May, Ebersol called me into a meeting at his hotel suite in Beverly Hills. I didn't see it coming. He abruptly told me I was being removed from the studio host position and would be sent back out to call games. As had been the case working with Ahmad, I was back near the bottom of the play-by-play pecking order, working with lower-profile expert commentators—Todd Christensen, later Bob Golic—nice guys, but the network wasn't interested in them.

Oh, well, I would still have golf. I had earned a fair sampling of critical praise for sorting out all the scorekeeping twists and turns covering the Ryder Cup at an English course named The Belfry in the fall of 1993 (as Marv Albert filled in for me as host of *NFL Live* Sunday). In 1994 I worked to get more comfortable in the job, a task made a bit more complicated by the ongoing collapse of my own game. Golf was pretty much the only network sports arena where the people on the telecast were expected to play respectably for professional credibility. I thought I could handle that part, having been number two on my high school golf team in Miami and posting a remarkably low handicap for a 17-year-old at Hendersonville Country Club in North Carolina, where my late father was once club champion and course record holder.

But I hadn't played much since beer had taken over my life for my first three years of college in Chapel Hill. I had just STOPPED playing. In '93 when the network set up an early date for me to play with PGA Tour commissioner Deane Beman at TPC Sawgrass in Ponte Vedra, Florida, I was a disaster. No point in even guessing what the score was because of the gracious and necessary mulligans I was given to keep us moving at a socially acceptable speed. After we had played a couple of rounds over the years, O'Neil assured the network that I was good enough. It was nothing to write home about, but it was probably 15 or 20 strokes better than what Beman saw in the wind at Ponte Vedra. I might have been dead from that moment, Ryder Cup or no Ryder Cup.

The next two years became a blur, during which I lost the golf tele-cast, watched my status in the NBC NFL hierarchy further diminish, and poured too much money into business ventures I shouldn't have tried. I also learned that Bryant Gumbel would host HBO's soon-to-debut long-form sports magazine that I had been discussing with their executives and producers for years in anticipation of filling that role.

The series title was *Real Sports*, scheduled to start early in 1995, and in December they got around to telling me officially that I would be "senior reporter" on the show. At first, I wanted to turn it down. But my agent simply said, "Jim, stop cutting your own throat. You'll do great at this. By any standard other than yours it is a great job. The public doesn't know what they promised you."

He was right, and in the first three years of the series I won two Em-mys for Best Sports Reporting. During that time, I made a somewhat unexpected pile of money—more than $700,000 in royalties—from a sun-glasses infomercial I hosted. It was probably a primary reason for HBO to reach for Bryant and his established journalist credibility. I should have seen that coming. My agent should have seen it coming. But maybe he was beginning to wonder when the stream of healthy commissions was going to run aground under the weight of my moves not approved by my coun-selor Arthur Kaminsky.

23

Trial of the Century

n June 1994 I was shooting one of those infomercials for Eagle Eyes at the Riviera Country Club in Los Angeles when I heard Nicole Brown Simpson had been brutally murdered.

I was on the practice tee at Riviera with a crew and a makeup artist and a limo driver, and sometime around noon someone piped up and said, "Oh, my God, did you hear about Nicole Simpson?" I was 45 years old, and it was the first time I had ever heard the name of a friend in a sentence that included "murdered."

If it had been challenging to get up for gushing lines about gimmick sunglasses before that, it was now a lot harder. I raced home to see what my news anchor wife had gathered about Nicole and began trying to focus on my professional obligations—the most challenging two weeks of the year, hosting HBO's live five hours of weekday tennis coverage from Wimbledon.

That was Monday. Tuesday, I foolishly told reporters from the *New York Times* and *USA Today*: "No way, not our guy, not capable of that and

I'm sure he was still in love with her." Wednesday, I saw those quotes prominently included on front-page articles about the murder while boarding an overnight flight to London. Thursday, I checked in to the Athenaeum Hotel in Piccadilly, got some rest, did some shopping, and read tennis until I fell asleep.

Friday, I was up early for the ride out to Wimbledon and all-day rehearsals. The HBO production compound on the grounds of the All England Club was directly connected to NBC's operation, so in a normal workday I would see and speak to Dick Enberg and his expert commentators along with our HBO group: Billie Jean King, John Lloyd, Martina Navratilova, Barry MacKay, and Larry Merchant among them. Needless to say, one topic overshadowed the conversation that Friday. Billie Jean recalled being around O.J. and me together at the ABC *Superstars* special 19 years before. On one thing we were unanimous: No one wanted to learn that O.J. was the killer. Everyone wanted, and hoped for, a different answer.

The two American networks shared a commissary. Lunch was like a group meeting as all the on-air talking dogs along with executives and producers and directors kibitzed about the murder—and about the husband under suspicion who most of us knew well as a friend and colleague.

I thought it would take a few more days for what had happened to Nicole to become clear. On the ride back to town I focused on the mountain of tennis material I needed to absorb before Monday morning. I turned on CNN to catch up and saw a helicopter, live, tracking O.J.'s white Ford Bronco driving at abnormally slow speeds down the 405 freeway. I sagged back onto the sofa with a few deep breaths to steady myself. Then I began trying to come to grips with the obvious implication that a friend *might have* viciously sliced up two people.

To fully understand the resistance on the part of many in the sports and entertainment community to the obvious implications of the Bronco escape fantasy, you need to know that O.J. Simpson was friendly to many people and willing to share his fame and sometimes over-the-top personality with others who were not as gifted by ability and fate as he was.

That was behind my reflexive urge to repay him when questioned about the murders by the *New York Times* and *USA Today*. I couldn't imagine any of his friends saying anything different to reporters than what I had said, and few did about a story growing darker by the day.

Leading to the criminal trial, there were some left in O.J.'s world who still believed he couldn't possibly be guilty. Personally, I wished with all my heart I could bond with that sentiment, but I just couldn't. To me, it seemed obvious: If he didn't commit the crime, why was he hiding in the back seat of the Bronco while lifetime friend Al Cowlings drove off down the 405 to nowhere? Only one answer worked.

It was a tough Wimbledon, always a tough gig for me, because I was more a student of tennis than an expert, and therefore I was susceptible to mistakes during five-hour telecasts with no commercial breaks. Sometimes, when it rained, there were no matches either, which would become extended periods of an on-set tennis version of *The View*, or if you prefer another metaphor, of cable television election coverage. I was the central figure, the ringmaster, the content motivator of everything, and doing that while a significant percentage of my mind was still distracted by O.J.'s flight.

To add to the distraction, Bree came to London during the second week, bringing her five-year-old daughter and our two-year-old son into the hotel suite, diminishing my sleep and the recharging of my battery. When the tournament was finally over, we traveled back through Bree's family homeland of upper Minnesota, where her whole family was eager to discuss O.J., O.J., nothing but O.J.

Late on Monday, July 4, the four of us boarded a United Airlines flight from Minneapolis to Los Angeles. Also on the flight was rock and roller Tommy James of "Crystal Blue Persuasion" fame. He correctly perceived my connection to the story and grilled me with questions I could answer. Everyone on the plane seemed aware that the trial process was to begin the next day with a hearing for the defense and prosecutors to ask questions of an unusual witness: O.J.'s housemate from nowhere, Kato Kaelin.

On the flight I began feeling sick. Dry throat turning sore, the beginnings of chills and fever, sweaty without really being hot, all symptoms I perceived as logical flu or cold, my reward for an exhausting three weeks in a high-pressure enclosure. By the time we all reached our house in the Hollywood Hills, I was deathly ill. I went upstairs and fell into bed, leaving Bree with reorganizing and feeding the kids and entertaining them for a couple of hours before putting them to bed. I was too out of it to even notice when she finally crawled in beside me.

———————

The trial dominated the news for months. I had some distractions. Fights to call on HBO, NFL games and golf tournaments to cover on NBC, and tee times with friends and new acquaintances, some at places where I had played with O.J. before the murders.

For a long time during this period, I wondered if I might be asked by the defense to testify as a character witness on O.J.'s behalf. And there was one moment that seemed to answer that question, when in late summer I was in Beverly Hills for the annual Taste of LA setup, a great opportunity to mingle with LA elites and sample high-end restaurant food. Bree and I were standing on the west side of Rodeo Drive just below Santa Monica Boulevard when I glanced across the street and spotted a distinctive threesome of men walking my way—O.J.'s criminal attorney Robert Shapiro;

his ICM (International Creative Management) agent, Jack Gilardi; and a Beverly Hills antique dealer with whom I had played golf in groups set up by Simpson. They were looking my way, and for a moment I considered whether there was an inconspicuous escape route, but it was too late.

After the obligatory greetings, Shapiro got right to the point. "So, Lamps, we were just talking about you the other day." I waited for the punch line. "At Parker Center." The jail where O.J. was held. "Are you around? You aren't planning to leave town anytime soon, are you?" I gave him the answer he was looking for. "No." And just like that, they were off and down the street, setting me up for three or four weeks of edgy sleep. Character witness. There was no other way to interpret that. I wouldn't have been required to testify; I could always say no. O.J. was my friend, but the evidence unfolding at trial was troubling.

But after a few weeks passed, I began to breathe easier. It was clear from the body language surrounding the trial that the defense felt it was two touchdowns ahead and merely had to run out the clock. Character witnesses would be nothing more than an unnecessary waste of time.

On October 3, 1995, I was lifting at Bally's gym, which was packed with every form of apparatus in use, late in morning rush hour. Suddenly, the atmosphere changed from purposeful mental isolation to communal anticipation, with dozens of people gathered around a small TV screen set up on a folding chair. We were all in Judge Lance Ito's courtroom for the long-awaited verdict. It all happened quickly, with a far more perfunctory feel than I would have expected. Some people gasped, some groaned, many more cheered, and I was shocked enough to feel the breath leave my body in a way that suggested it wouldn't be back soon. Two words—"not guilty"—and it was over. Or so I thought.

I was stunned. I had worked so hard in my mind to accommodate O.J.'s obvious guilt that I didn't know exactly how to feel about being up-ended. I needed someone to explain it to me. And instantly I realized I knew only one person in Hollywood who had seen every single minute of the trial. Someone who played golf all day, went home to Mulholland Drive and dined each night, then sat down to watch the trial activities his household staff had dutifully recorded while he was out. Every witness, every legal maneuver, every motion, every day.

I ran out without changing out of my workout clothes. The drive from Bally's to the Lakeside Country Club might have taken seven minutes. I parked, raced into the caddie shack, and blurted out, "Where's Jack?" The answer was maybe seven, maybe eight. I grabbed an empty cart and raced, as fast as I could, to the par-four seventh hole, arriving just in time to watch quietly as Jack Nicholson, a good putter, rolled in an eight-footer for what would go onto his scorecard as a par. He turned around and smiled.

"Whatcha doin', Lamp?"

"Jack, they have a verdict!"

"Really?" A slight pause. "Not guilty."

Stunning to me. "How the hell did you know that?"

"Lamp, come on. No witness, no murder weapon, nine Black jurors. They've been sequestered forever. They wanted to go to lunch."

"But, Jack, I can't believe it. I can't believe he got off."

An interruption, with raising volume. "Got off? What do you mean got off?"

"Well, he won't go to prison. He's free. No penalty. He got off."

"Lamp, mark my words, he didn't get off. No one gets off from this. The life he is about to have, nobody would want it. You couldn't stand it, neither could I. It will be awful. Believe me, Lamp, he didn't get off. That's the last thing that could have happened."

And every day that has passed since then has proven Jack's point.

In the ensuing years I came close to having contact with O.J., but it never happened. Once he entered a party after an Oscar De La Hoya fight in Las Vegas, but I had already left the room. Later he attended a Roy Jones fight in Miami, but I had a tight schedule to catch a late flight back to Los Angeles and left the auditorium in a hurry. So 30 years after the verdict, no brush with the friend whom I once called "Juicy."

What would I have said? I hoped I could bring myself to hark back to how considerate he was to me when I was functionally nobody in his world and he was O.J. Simpson. I hoped that I could have thanked him for the memories. But could I have done that in good conscience in the face of the horrifying crime I believe he committed?

It never happened. Almost a year after Simpson revealed he was dealing with prostate cancer, he died on April 10, 2024. He never served time for the murder of his wife and her friend but spent nine years in jail for other, unrelated charges. As Nicholson foretold, the good part of his life as one of the most famous athletes and celebrities in the world had ended long before that.

24

The Lead Dog

Jack said "Longevity is lovability" (Courtesy of Jim Lampley)

It Happened!

As 1996 began, I was seeking to recover from a series of career disappointments, some of them the product of my own misjudgments and bad behaviors. I had lost the NBC Sports 18th hole golf tower and NFL studio in the preceding year and a half, and I suspected I had cost myself the host chair for *Real Sports* at HBO by taking easy money to do an infomercial. My high-profile marriage to news anchor Bree Walker was a rock pile, and she had lost her anchor chair at KCBS-TV. By the end of the summer, we were done with Hollywood and took our two kids off to year-round living in our ski house in Park City, Utah.

The fresh air felt like our only chance at redemption. We were now too jaded and wounded by Hollywood life to look at each other with a straight face. Park City was Hollywood only for one month a year, when the Sundance Film Festival took over the town. That one month shouldn't be enough to kill us. But just to make sure we could maximize Sundance, I shelled out a monstrous sum of money to fulfill a foolish dream to have my own restaurant, a bar and bistro named Lakota in a can't-miss location fewer than 20 feet from the Park City Mountain town lift.

I dreamed of becoming a great skier and dominating the restaurant scene. In the next two years I would have time only to slightly improve my sloppy skiing and launch Lakota well enough to become a fixture on the downtown circuit. And the tumult of Hollywood did not give way to greater serenity, so I sold Lakota. My frequent travel and continuing TV exposures made Bree increasingly agitated and eager to be back on camera.

No golf and no NFL studio meant a lower public profile, but amid reporting assignments from *Real Sports* and boxing matches and then Wimbledon, there was still no shortage of travel and work. As I made final preparations for the 1996 Olympics in Atlanta, Brooke was coming from London, where her mother now lived, to join me. We met in New York, where on Thursday, July 11, former World Boxing Organization (WBO) world heavyweight champion Riddick Bowe was looking to set up another title shot against Poland's undefeated Andrew Golota at Madison Square Garden.

Brooke's original plan was to come to the fight alone, and through HBO I secured a ticket for her to sit in the front row right behind my ringside table. But I got a message from her that she wanted to bring an old school friend from upper New Jersey, Mike Kopech, to the fight. She would take potluck with the seat location, knowing that a second front-row seat would at that point be impossible. I wouldn't know for sure where she and Mike were, but they were teenagers, so I wasn't that worried.

The Garden was jammed, a cross-cultural battleground for Bowe and Golota's distinctly different clienteles. The fight was flabbergasting; under-dog Golota constantly beat Bowe to the punch and ripped power shots to his chin and rib cage. Through six mostly one-sided rounds, Golota had built a lead marred only by his own repeated low blows. He was warned in the second round and penalized a point in round three for hitting Bowe in the crotch. In the sixth and seventh rounds Golota landed two more flagrantly illegal below-the-belt shots, his fourth and fifth of the fight, and referee Wayne Kelly abruptly disqualified him, touching off a riot.

Golota's fans were incensed that an official's judgment had blocked their man from a chance to fight for the heavyweight crown. They were affronted that he was being ruthlessly mugged. A member of Bowe's en-tourage leaped over the ring ropes and ran across to Golota's corner to assault the Polish fighter with a 1996-size walkie-talkie. The butt of the heavy instrument repeatedly thudded into the top of Golota's skull. And in a matter of seconds, there were fistfights all around the ring and a free-for-all inside it, seemingly every man for himself.

Larry Merchant, George Foreman, and I kept our seats at ringside. Then as the surrounding chaos built and we could see violence spreading in front of us, we stood up. With my headset microphone still on I was describing events in the ring, suddenly including the removal of Golota's trainer, Lou Duva, looking severely stricken, on a gurney. At about that moment our announcer location with all its necessary audio engineering gear toppled over. And as I replaced my headset to continue covering the riot, I could hear Foreman, in a calm voice, urging a couple of would-be entrants to the rumble in the ring to reconsider their urge.

"You don't want to climb up in there. You're only going to get hurt. Turn around and go back to your seats," Big George advised.

As I turned away from the ring to look at them, I found George's huge left arm jutting out across my body like a safety barrier, protecting me while I kept talking. It occurred to me we had performed our show opening on camera from a high platform about a third of the way back into the lower-deck seating area. There would be audio gear there, and I would be able to see more clearly what was going on. I knew Merchant would want to stay in the thick of things, and he would have Foreman for protection.

From high up on the camera platform, the heart of the problem became visible. The uniformed Madison Square Garden security guards were classic rent-a-cop types, unarmed and ill-equipped to deal with real violence. People were attacking each other with folding chairs. If there were any true New York City police in the area, they were not yet in evidence inside the arena.

The reports I heard later regarding the length of time it took for a police presence to materialize ranged from 7 minutes to more than 15 minutes. I wasn't counting, I was reporting. Merchant lobbed in a ringside observation. Foreman kept playing peacemaker. After something like order had been restored, HBO Sports executive producer Ross Greenburg got on his internal microphone and urged me to begin summing the whole thing up, with a reminder to cover what had happened in the boxing match and get us to a "good night" conclusion. The last thing he said was, "And whatever personal comment you want to make about all this, feel free to let it rip."

And that was the moment it first occurred to me Brooke was in the crowd somewhere. It shook me. I followed Ross's instruction, and as I looked into the camera to say good night, I told the audience, "I've got a sixteen-year-old daughter in here somewhere. I've got to find her."

A striking way to close a landmark show, all real, all natural. Brooke was fine, thank heavens, because the best tickets HBO could provide her at the last minute were up in the second deck. They watched the riot but were not in it.

The following day we flew to Atlanta for the Olympics. I was again co-hosting the late-night segments with Hannah Storm. Brooke would go to some events such as high-prestige track and field with some of my Hollywood entertainment friends, notably Jack Nicholson and film producer James L. Brooks. But most of the time she chose to be in the late-night office or the control room, watching me work at close range, enjoying her friendships with the large squadron of young staffers at NBC. She knew everyone from Dick Ebersol down to the rookie runners and had clear pictures of what most of them did.

Our daily journeys from the Renaissance Hotel to and from the broadcast center were on public transportation. Frequently in the first week following, total strangers turned to us and asked, "Is this the girl? This is your daughter?" And repeatedly she would recite her version of the story I had been telling the preceding Saturday night. She got her own first taste of being a public figure, and I was thinking she enjoyed it, but not too much. And by the beginning of the Olympic Games that weekend, massive news stories wiped the slate clean.

For the second time in four years, we went to the opening ceremony together. Like everyone in the crowd we watched the entry of the flame in rapt anticipation of the answer to a carefully kept secret: Who would light the torch on American soil? Brooke was a little ahead of me in nailing the answer: the man who had entertained her with magic and card tricks at the Boxing

Writers Association of America dinner eight years before, Muhammad Ali. The sight of Ali in the spotlight above an epic staircase to the top rim of the stadium, trembling in the grip of his advancing Parkinson's but proudly igniting the Olympic flame, was beyond breathtaking. It was deeply personal, and sure to be unforgettable, and eerily typical of all our father-and-daughter experiences. My boyhood hero, her poet laureate, and still as famous and meaningful as any human being alive. It was a refreshing and rejuvenating way for the Atlanta Games to begin, for Brooke and me, for NBC Sports chief Ebersol, who had helped to mastermind the plan behind the scenes, and ironically, for the sport of boxing, which eight days after the stain of Bowe-Golota saw its own living saint bathed in the global spotlight.

———

Eight days after that something happened that made the Bowe-Golota riot seem trivial. Hannah and I were seated on the late-night set just past 1 AM on July 27 when word came in that a bomb had gone off in a place named Centennial Park, near to the broadcast center. A crowd of thousands had assembled there for a free concert, and there were numerous reports of injuries.

John McGuinness instantly became a news producer, and Hannah and I converted to news-anchor mode. And we held our own, because no broadcasters are as experienced in dealing with extemporaneously developing stories and live adjustments as sportscasters are. We did what we knew how to do. Eventually we bore the sadness of reporting that a 44-year-old woman from Albany, Georgia, had been killed by a nail that penetrated her skull, and a 40-year-old Turkish cameraman had died of a heart attack. Eleven other people were hospitalized, among 111 wounded. Sometime past 3 AM Tom Brokaw, the central face of NBC News, hurried onto the set to replace us.

For the second time in three weekends, I had instantaneously put my news anchor background into play in the coverage of something more serious than sports competition. For the second time it was widely noticed, and Hannah and I fielded congratulations from everyone around us in the broadcast center. Maybe too many congratulations. Maybe there in the bosom of NBC, where I had suffered embarrassing losses in the two preceding years, I was too eager to bask in the limelight.

On Monday I answered questions for *USA Today* about what had happened on the set Sunday night. In a conscience-free burst of self-approval, I unleashed a barrage of damaging quotes suggesting that Hannah had recognized my news anchor–based primacy in that situation and had in effect deferred to me on the set. Even I knew that wasn't really true. The most stupidly salacious quote was partially reproduced in the headline: "To make that situation work, one or the other of us has to be the lead dog."

At the broadcast center was a message calling me into Dick Ebersol's office. There was no available defense to be mounted, I had stupidly dishonored Hannah, the sports anchor I respected beyond all others, and my apologies to her, though she gracefully purported to accept them, were empty. I felt a brand of shame I had never before experienced in my career or my personal life. I limped through the rest of the Atlanta Games, but the whole time I felt enclosed by my self-constructed black cloud.

Two moments distracted me enough to lift some of the gloom. The first occurred later that week when I approached the men's room in the hallway outside the late-night office and noticed a gaggle of large men in blue suits standing outside the entrance door. I walked past them, strode to the urinal, and as I began my business there, glanced to my right to encounter a famous acquaintance.

Shortly after I had been fired from my KCBS-TV news anchoring job in 1992 I was contacted by Bill Clinton's presidential campaign to anchor with him a live fundraiser that was televised in five California cities. We had spent several hours together in the greenroom and on the set, two Southern boys raised on Southern politics with a great deal in common. Now we greeted each other shoulder to shoulder at the urinal, he on the way to his second term in the White House, me wondering what the next misadventure in my seemingly foundering career would be. Under the cir-cumstances, there was no handshake.

The second redemptive moment sprang spontaneously from my eldest daughter. A swimming star of the Atlanta Games was freestyle sprinter Gary Hall Jr. He was a second-generation Olympian, and I had inter-viewed his father on the field at the closing ceremony in Montreal 20 years before on the night when he was chosen to carry the United States flag. Now his son was a second-week hero in Atlanta, having anchored two re-lay gold medals and winning two individual silvers. He attracted attention with his pool deck theatrics, arriving in robe and boxing trunks, shadow-boxing and performing calisthenics before he swam. With piercing blue eyes and chlorine-blond hair, he was movie-star handsome, a condition not unknown to him.

It was a standard reflex for the late-night show to reel in and debrief all the American stars who stayed for the closing ceremony. And at the moment when Gary Hall Jr. was brought into the broadcast center, word spread among the college-age and close-to-college-age women on the NBC staff. Dozens packed the narrow hallway outside our telecast studio in the hope of getting a word or a photo with Hall. But there was a back entrance to the studio, and the center of attention was sneaked onto the set without contacting his assembled admirers. He sat alone on a sofa and waited for Hannah and me to get made up and brought in. And that process hadn't even yet begun.

In the control room, producer McGuinness urgently looked around, announcing to the team, "Hey, we need someone to keep this guy engaged. Who can go in there and talk with him while he awaits Hannah and Jim?"

And as a half dozen other female voices immediately rose to the task, Mc-Guinness's eyes lit on the one silent female in the room.

"Brooke, go onto the set and keep him entertained."

It was the last thing the older women, most all of them actually employed by NBC, wanted to hear, and there was a group groan as the only 16-year-old girl among them obediently rose from her back-row chair and slipped into the studio. She sat down facing the matinee idol of the Atlanta Olympics and began to make small talk.

But the microphones on the set were shut down at that moment, so the control room was getting a silent movie for a minute or so. A cacophony of voices loudly urged the audio engineer, "Pot them up! We want to hear this." Audio looked at McGuinness, and he nodded.

It was truly small talk. But pretty soon, Hall got to the obvious question, who was this teenager and why did she have access to a studio at the Olympics? And when Brooke had filled in that blank, he asked the most logical question imaginable.

"So, do you want to work in sports television like your dad?"

Instantly, reflexively, with no necessary consideration: "Oh, no, never. I've seen the dark side of this business."

The crew in the control room was dumbfounded. "Oh, my God, did she really just say that? Where did she come up with that thought?"

Brooke was already something of a curiosity in the NBC Olympics culture due to her omnipresence in Barcelona and Atlanta. Now, at least for the small group in that control room, she was a legend. And though some who heard her manifesto might have doubted it, she knew whereof she spoke. In nearly 30 years since Atlanta, she has never come anywhere close to working in my world, and now as senior director for the Gagosian galleries in New York City, she clearly never will.

Two weeks after the closing ceremony, I saw my penalty for the incredibly stupid "lead dog" comments. Ebersol issued a production schedule that showed I was headed to Daytona Beach to cover the US cheerleading championships. CHEERLEADING? It wasn't a misprint. If I had harbored any doubt that my career in commercial network television sports was now thoroughly on the rocks, there it was in black and white.

"Lead dog"? I felt like a dead dog. Beyond cheerleading I knew I could look forward to a dreary fall schedule of tail-end NFL games, and my chances of working at the Sydney Olympics in 2000 were dead. Just dead. The contract would expire before then.

I agonized. I lost sleep. I ruminated about how to lift myself up out of the funk I had created. I knew one person who had faced such emptiness in his life and somehow conquered it. I needed some more Nicholson knowledge. Most of the world could never have known his story, but I did. So I picked up my cell phone and called Jack.

I had met him in an art gallery years before and we struck up a conversation about boxing. Now we shared a financial manager, had many friendships in common, and played countless hours of golf together. In golf cart after golf cart I interviewed him and marveled at his wisdom, his recognition of the degree to which we are all subject to inexplicable fate. He knew the counterintuitive narrative of how, after waiting for a decade for the match to be struck in his acting career, he had given up in favor of becoming a full-time producer, only for that path to reverse when another actor had a fight with Dennis Hopper and gave up his role in *Easy Rider*. More than anyone else I knew, Jack Nicholson was in touch with the reality that what is meant to be is meant to be, and we accept it or live in disappointment.

I had spent many hours in Jack's Mulholland Drive living room talking about art, about golf, about him, but never before with a total focus on me. We sat down and he listened as I spelled out the desolation I felt and the dreariness I saw in the emerging photo of my career. I asked him how actors, uninsured in their ambitions, lacking guaranteed contracts and continuing assignments, held on to their personal security when things went bad. And in a matter of a few minutes, Jack rescued me emotionally and saved my career.

"The first part of this, Lamp, is the oldest lesson in what I do: There are no lesser parts, only lesser actors. Whatever assignment they want to give you, even if it is the cheerleading championships, your job is to approach it proudly and perform the task as the greatest in the world ever to do it. There's no other choice. Muscle up; something else will come your way."

I thought about it and tried to digest it. There was no point in disputing it. I already had a plane ticket to Daytona Beach. He added a bit more.

"You still have boxing, and you are the best in the world at that. You work for the most prestigious network in television, at HBO where they aren't selling soap. Focus on what you do best and trust it to take care of you."

That felt better. And then the clincher.

"The second part is something you probably haven't even thought of yet. You're only 47. But take this to heart and never forget it: In any public platform, longevity is lovability. Hang in and do your best. If you can stay around long enough, they've got no fucking choice other than to love you."

So almost 30 years later I can unequivocally say Jack was right; 30 years later and still with an enviable niche in the business of describing sports events and personalities on television, I thank him every day; 30 years later Jack's words of wisdom ring in my ears, a code for staying sane in a business that can drive you to do crazy, self-destructive things, as I know all too well.

25

"It Happened!"

The moment Moorer let George knock him out
(The Ring Magazine/Getty)

A s the 1990s continued and George Foreman's products kept
selling, he was meticulously picking heavyweight opponents and fight opportunities that kept his name in the ring

discussion and reminded the division's top competitors he was still out there, still active.

And on April 22, 1994, he and I, with Larry Merchant, called an upset victory at the top of the division, champion Evander Holyfield's majority-decision loss to unbeaten but largely unheralded Michael Moorer, who was 26 at the time.

Moorer became history's first southpaw heavyweight champ and intelligently cast his net for the opponent with whom he could combine the highest income-earning possibility and the logical expectation he would win and go forward to other title defenses. The answer was obvious. Moorer vs. Foreman was set for November 5, 1994, at the MGM Grand in Las Vegas. George was a big underdog, but he would have a chance to win back the heavyweight championship he had lost to Muhammad Ali at the Rumble in the Jungle in Zaire.

Moorer had dictated the late rounds against Holyfield to win the crown. He had a strong amateur pedigree and was groomed on the way up by the renowned Emanuel Steward at the boxing-revered Kronk Gym in Detroit. For this fight he was trained by another star, Cus D'Amato protégé and former Mike Tyson instructor Teddy Atlas. Since George was vacating his customary HBO chair to enter the ring, veteran expert Gil Clancy signed on to call the fight with Larry and me.

In the opening on camera, I asked Gil what chance he gave to Foreman to spring the upset, and the two-word answer was "very little." At 45 years old, George would become the oldest ever to win the title if he pulled it off. He climbed into the ring wearing the same trunks he had on against Ali in Kinshasha, 20 years and six days before. And he had been trained for this fight by the same man who had trained Ali, another legend, Angelo Dundee.

Though an underdog, George was making it clear he understood the power of mythology and symbolism. For the opening of our telecast, he agreed to recite the lyrics of "The Impossible Dream."

By this time in our relationship I had grown comfortable enough to engage George in frank discussions. He had volunteered advice on some intensely personal subjects—marital conflicts, parenting challenges, rough spots in my relationship with NBC—so I felt no compunction now about talking to him about his career. He knew I admired his strong-mindedness and gave him credit for wisdom outside the ring. And though I had expected he might take time away from ringside commentary to train for the fight, that hadn't turned out to be the case. We covered a Lennox Lewis fight in London in late September and a Pernell Whitaker date in Norfolk, Virginia, in October.

On one of those occasions, I pulled him aside in an idle moment and asked a frank question: "George, how exactly do you plan to beat Moorer? I mean, he's a southpaw, he's a mover, Holyfield had trouble finding him, and Evander has quicker feet than you do. So what's the plan?" I asked him at least twice, maybe more.

The answer was simple and adamant: "Jim, you watch. There will come a moment, late in the fight, he will come and stand in front of me and let me knock him out."

"Let you knock him out? What does that mean?"

"You heard me. Just watch. When it happens, remember what I told you."

If he wasn't George Foreman I might have passed it off. But he was who he was, and I knew he didn't take it lightly. If there was one thing I had learned working with him, he was a serious man. He never said things he didn't mean. Though I wasn't dwelling on it, the words were there in the framework of my approach as Merchant, Clancy, and I sat down to call the four-fight card that night, November 5, 1994, in Las Vegas.

Moorer and Atlas had a solid plan. The champ was sticking his jab and moving to his right, away from George's still-formidable right hand. Both corners were businesslike, efficient, and calm. Scorer Harold Lederman might have found a round or two to give to George, but by the time we arrived at round 10, Moorer had a mathematical hold on the lead and the fight. Logic said George would have to sell out, take a risk of some sort to try to land a big shot. Otherwise, the predictable result was at hand.

Later I looked back on tape and realized that in the first minute of the 10th round, George had thrown a series of wide-sweeping left hooks, a punch he hadn't featured in the fight up to that point. A few of the hooks landed, and in retrospect the purpose was to move Moorer over just a step or two in his stance, so Foreman could strike him with a right hand thrown straight from the shoulder for maximum power.

A classic jab and solid right-hand combination put Moorer down midway through the round, and he was nowhere near beating the count. If in fact Moorer had let George knock him out, he had been set up to do it by one of the greatest heavyweight punchers in history.

When the count reached 10, I had to find the right words to curate a moment of unforgettable boxing history, just as had been the case in Tokyo in the Buster Douglas–Mike Tyson fight four years and nine months before. This time I had better, less prosaic material to work with, thanks to what George himself had told me to expect.

"It happened! It happened!" I shouted into the mic without much more of an explanation.

I called fights for 31 years, from 1987 to 2018. I've never bothered to count them up, but I know there were hundreds, and that is by far the most famous call I delivered. It describes what took place between Foreman and Moorer. It describes what followed in 1974 when I traveled from Chapel Hill to Birmingham for a pipe-dream interview to seek a once-in-a-lifetime network television opportunity.

It happened, and boxing fans I don't know still yell that to me in airports, on the streets of New York, and along the Vegas Strip.

Beyond that, I have no further explanation of how it did happen.

26

The Last Round

"I Think About Emanuel Almost Every Day"
(Left: Courtesy of Jim Lampley. Right: Courtesy of Jeff Julian)

Τhe cable host chair in the Sydney Olympics that summer of 2000 proved to be the loneliest experience of my career. Much of it was my own doing that I was trying to fix by including my family wherever and whenever I could. In 1999, my 12-year-old daughter, Victoria, made her first-ever trip with me on an assignment to England for a featherweight fight between British star Prince Naseem Hamed and a nondescript opponent named Paul Ingle. I picked up Victoria in London, where she lived with her mother, and we went on to Manchester for the HBO event.

Family folklore had the name Lampley as being endemic to northern England. The day before the fight, we went sightseeing around Manchester with several graveyards on our list. Sure enough, at the Episcopal cemetery in the middle of the city, there it was: a granite gravestone with the name "LAMPLEY" from the 14th century. We found a handful of them. Victoria saw it as a reason to be proud of her name. I saw it as another gift from boxing.

Arriving in Sydney, I was alone again. While the rest of the NBC troops bunked in a glamorous downtown hotel near the beautiful broadcast center with a constant view of the architecturally magnificent opera house that adorned the bay, I moved farther out of the city to a remote apartment complex where only a handful of us, the cable-channel group, were housed. My on-air hours were mostly overnight, and only infrequently did I see a visitor or a guest. After all, who wanted to celebrate a medal-winning performance by going to a sterile television studio at three or four o'clock in the morning?

The heart of my job was to be smooth, professional, familiar to viewers who had seen me at Olympics going back 24 years, and to effectively speak the language of television broadcasts Dick Ebersol had helped establish. That began when Ebersol was the ABC Olympics researcher working for

Roone Arledge and Jim McKay in 1968. It wouldn't necessarily have been easy for just anyone, but it was something that now came naturally to me.

I kept my head down and my mouth shut because I was still trying to polish my prominence on a new and prestigious network, HBO. I had already returned to the States, but HBO had such a strong humanitarian culture that after the 2001 Lennox Lewis-Hasim Rahman fight in South Africa the crew and brass visited with Nelson Mandela at his home in Johannesburg. I regretted missing that!

————————

It was in no way surprising that I wound up with increasing studio roles in later Olympics. I was the daytime host and at night the cable-channel hockey host at Salt Lake City in 2002, and daytime host in Athens in 2004, Torino in 2006, and Beijing in 2008, where my son Aaron (with Bree Walker) was helping me through the awful darkness and smog that had engulfed the industrial city on his first business trip with me. I was distraught the conditions would seriously hamper our outside camera shots that were a big part of the opening ceremony. I went to the broadcast center, where there were no windows, while 17-year-old Aaron checked out Beijing.

In about an hour, my cell phone rang. It was Aaron, who said two words: "Step outside!" I was baffled by his order but the instant I pushed open the big metal door, I was in bright sunlight and a clear-blue sky. Aaron smiled ear to ear and hugged me. We learned that the Chinese government had ordered thousands of workers to go home and shut down their plants, clearing the soot and smog so they could fulfill their ambition of hosting the "greatest show on the planet." Since then, and for the rest of my life, I will hear Aaron say "step outside."

Beijing was my 14th and last Olympics assignment on six networks, counting over the air and cable. I have been told many times by various sources and authorities that it is a record for Olympics appearances by an American broadcaster. I take their word for it.

After 2008, new management at NBC Sports had other plans for my on-air hours. So Beijing marked my goodbye to the Olympic Games. The overall experience had lasted 32 years, and it was striking to realize the two most thrilling and memorable moments were Winter Olympics based: Franz Klammer's 1976 downhill run in Innsbruck, the first Olympics I ever attended, and the Miracle on Ice four years later. In both cases, I was more or less thrown in at the last minute. It was impossible to imagine how, from a sports-lover perspective, I could ever have been luckier. And 44 years after Lake Placid that remains indelibly true.

I was on the doorstep of 60 years old. As a television sports commentator I had been around the world and back several times, difficult even for the most learned fans to conjure a sport or an event I had never touched. I was confident about calling boxing matches, which had emerged now as my central on-air job, for as long as HBO wanted me in that role. I was developing a business and personal friendship with the executive who ran the entertainment side of HBO, a Los Angeles–based brainiac named Mike Lombardo, and his superior, copresident Richard Plepler.

My cherished longtime agent Art Kaminsky died in 2013 after he was incapacitated by an extended illness. With the help of my new agent in Los Angeles, Nick Khan, I produced an independent feature film, a satirical spoof named *Welcome to Hollywood*, which debuted and aired on Cinemax, the wholly owned subsidary network to HBO. Then came the documentary *On Freddie Roach*, about the esteemed boxing trainer, a cinema verité directed by the award-winning Peter Berg.

Khan was dynamic, indomitable, and busy. When I hooked up with him around the time of the Athens Olympics, he insisted I hire a manager named Michael Price because my ambitions as a producer would require day-to-day attention, and Nick would not have time for that. It meant paying two commissions, but Nick was right, and with the clock running now on a career that had begun when I was 25, I didn't want to miss any chances.

By May 2012 I had a semimonthly magazine series, *The Fight Game*, airing in prime time on HBO. *TFG*, as the staff called it, was a thrilling outlet for my content hunger, my writing capacity, and my ongoing relationships with fighters and trainers. It aired for seven seasons and did a lot to strengthen my footprint and legacy in boxing.

When Muhammad Ali died in 2016, *TFG* was the base camp from which we produced, more or less overnight, a eulogy/memorial show that included tributes from George Foreman, LL Cool J, and Jack Nicholson, among others. Considering how my love affair with Cassius Clay had begun all the way back in the summer of 1960, an eventful 56 years before, I felt gifted to be in that position.

But years before Ali died, I had experienced a graphic demonstration of how we are all whipsawed by life's ups and downs. After some self-damaging misjudgments in my love life—specifically, the final grinding dissolution of my third marriage to my former news anchor partner Bree Walker, then a terribly mistaken liaison to a beauty-pageant type who had approached me with the expressed goal of becoming a boxing commentator—I felt I had bottomed out as a person. To make myself feel better, I joined a group that was cold-calling voters in Ohio and explaining why they should vote for Barack Obama.

At this time in 2008 I had been living in Del Mar in north San Diego County for about a decade, ever since my hip difficulties had made it pointless to live on a ski mountain in Park City. It was ill-advised to keep living alone because postsurgical trauma following a hip replacement had left me with a dislocation syndrome. Over a 10-year period the ball of my right hip exited the socket 17 times, always leaving me immobilized because the pain from any movement whatsoever was excruciating beyond description. In all 17 instances I was lucky enough to be with someone or able to reach my cell phone, and thankfully I never went into shock, eventually to dehydrate and die. I was lucky beyond logic and reason.

There were two key steps to my eventual salvation. The most important step had been to seek and find the right love interest and life partner to finally find permanence and emotional stability in a life which had for too long been a crapshoot.

So the hip fix could wait. I needed a valuable companion who could help my four children feel proud of their father. For the first time ever, and in my mind just for fun, I filled out the identity page for the online dating service Match.com. My profile description was couched in the lyrics of Jackson Browne, which I judged to be more literary than the classic songs I might otherwise have used. I specified that I was looking for someone dark-haired, dark-eyed, over 50 and willing to admit it, and I finished by establishing where I stood politically because the preferences my mother instilled in me are strong enough to affect face-to-face relationships.

I could write another book on the degree to which I hit the jackpot. Suffice to say from the first one-hour, get-acquainted conversation at a Mexican restaurant in Encinitas, Debra Schuss Clemens reinvented my existence, and she continues to do so to this day. I was under the false impression I had loved several women in my adult years. But I learned from Debra that true love and devotion were joyful disciplines I had never embraced with energetic commitment and responsibility, and 16 years later, she is still, hour by hour, teaching me and our seven adult children and 11 grandchildren how to love. And without her I suspect I would not still be alive.

As a native Long Islander and a lifelong fan of baseball and football, Debra was from the beginning no stranger to sports. She didn't have a lot of exposure to boxing, but she caught on fast to the intensely personal nature of the sport. And five times in the first few years of traveling to-gether, I dislocated my hip. So she grew accustomed to getting me quickly into the hands of emergency medicine and watching me walk out of hos-pitals. She knew I wouldn't last forever that way, and she helped me keep pushing to find a permanent solution.

Eventually an orthopedic surgeon at Torrey Pines Orthopedic Clinic located a Swiss surgeon who had created a preventive implement, a small cage, which could be surgically attached to the hip socket to prevent the ball from escaping its nook. On March 26, 2012, with no firm knowledge or expectation but in the face of Debra's command that to keep going without trying was personal malpractice, I underwent surgery for the in-stallation of the cage in San Diego. After 17 dislocations in the preceding 12 years, I have had none since.

Again, I would not be alive without her.

Four and a half years after we met, Debra and I assembled 72 of our closest friends and relatives in the backyard of our house overlooking the historic Del Mar racetrack and the Pacific Ocean for a wonderful wedding of her own planning and design, then danced in our large living room and all around the pool deck to my own carefully assembled rhythm-and-blues collection. My dear friend, the famous "Ready to Rumble" ring an-nouncer Michael Buffer, conducted particulars of the nuptials.

The gathering was a who's who of boxing, including among others Larry Merchant, Max Kellerman, and Emanuel Steward, who had become one of my best friends. Later in the evening, after the sun had set over the Pacific, Emanuel's girlfriend Anita Ruiz told Debra he was having fierce and unrecognizable stomach pains, and they would have to leave early. I went to find him at the front door and hugged and kissed him goodbye.

By the following weekend Emanuel had disappeared into oncology in a Detroit hospital.

By October 25 he was dead. I was five when my father died, so that was not a mature enough experience of grief for me to evaluate. When my mother died in 1985, I was so accustomed to recognizing her heart's vulnerability that I had prepared for it many times. I had grieved over my half-brother's death a few years before this, but to be honest his lifestyle at the end invited the worst and it came as no surprise, his suffering so immense that my first emotion was relief. I can honestly say I had never dealt with such a heart-wrenching loss as that of Emanuel Steward. It was 12 years ago, and I think about him almost every day.

———————

The 1971 giant-dollar bonanza of the first Ali-Frazier match ushered in the ultimate Holy Grail for the promoters and television executives who run boxing: two boxers of similar weight and identity who, over a period of time, become star attractions. The public waits for them to fight so the hunger for their moment of truth drives the audience demand and the price consumers are willing to pay to higher and higher levels.

It happened over and over for several years before the event finally began to coalesce: In a shopping center near my home in north San Diego County, in the lobby or the hallway of a casino hotel in Las Vegas or Atlantic City, in the airports I made my way through more than half the weekends of the year, sometimes at a social gathering with friends, or sometimes just randomly on the street, someone would ask me a question that became a repetitious mantra: "When are Floyd Mayweather and Manny Pacquiao going to fight each other?"

The question reflected a variety of conditions that are endemic to boxing and in some ways unique to boxing: that the sport is underorganized and appealingly or maddeningly entrepreneurial. There are governing bodies that issue rankings and distribute championship belts, which have a representative appeal for some fully inoculated fans and for the competitors who rise high enough in the hierarchy to seek them. Fans who have followed boxing for years grow accustomed to the vagaries that bring star fighters together far more scarcely than, say, the Celtics playing the 76ers or the Yankees playing the Red Sox. They get frustrated with waiting, and most of them grow impatient with the reality that captivatingly competitive matchups are dangled speculatively, sometimes interminably, until by some alchemy they have ripened to the point of inevitability. Sometimes they rot instead.

The so-called "governing bodies" in reality have precious little ability to "govern" boxers who have significant followings and can generate audiences at the gate and on television. The managers and promoters who advise the athletes generally insist they play their cards close to the vest. Genuine risk is more often avoided than embraced, at least until the money piles up so high it can no longer be resisted. Fans can do little other than wait for the perverse nature of an entrepreneurial sport to take its course.

For years there was seemingly an all-too-real possibility that the two greatest active boxers in the world might never wind up in the ring together.

One of them was an American raised in the sport by a father and an uncle who had meaningful professional ring careers of their own, the other a product of the wretchedly impoverished streets of a mostly unobserved metropolis in the Philippines. And this despite the plain fact that in a sport whose most vital verity is "styles make fights," they were visibly and compellingly made for each other. Pacquiao was a savage attacker with speed, skill, and knockout power in both hands. Mayweather was a consummate boxer with impenetrable defense and artistic offense. Devoted fans of either could make a case to friends and rivals as to why their man would win.

So when in 2007 Mayweather won an entertaining war of skills with the most well-known and popular American star of the sport, Oscar De

La Hoya, the buzz began in earnest. It seemed clear Pretty Boy Floyd was close to unbeatable for any other fighter at or near that matchup's weight level of 154 pounds. He had gradually and systematically cleared out all opposition at 135, 140, and 147 on the way to the larger De La Hoya. The only remaining globally recognizable target in his universe was Pacquiao, who had begun his professional career at age 16 weighing less than 100 pounds before eventually being invited to America in 2001 and winning a 122-pound title against a heavily favored South African star in Las Vegas.

If Mayweather has a pretty good story, Pacquiao's is epic, one of the most colorful and compelling legends in the entire history of the sport. Unequipped with an American pedigree and a successful amateur career, two factors that had helped facilitate Mayweather's still-unbeaten record, Pacquiao had fought a who's who of mostly Asian and Mexican boxers on his way to the top. But general sports fans were still learning about him when more than a year after Mayweather defeated De La Hoya, Pacquiao entered the same ring in Las Vegas to take on the same naturally larger American Olympian and matinee idol.

The point of the fight was clear. The Pride of the Philippines needed to compete effectively with his American opponent to prove he was big enough and good enough to be a threat to Mayweather. Many ring experts doubted he could pull it off. And the result was staggering. Though De La Hoya had fought well against Mayweather before fading in the late rounds and losing a close-enough decision the year before, the smaller Pacquiao annihilated the once-magnificent Golden Boy. The fight was a start-to-finish beatdown before De La Hoya's corner mercifully threw in the towel to stop it after eight rounds.

Manny Pacquaio, who in childhood had sold stolen cigarettes on the streets of General Santos city to survive, earned a reported $30 million from the pay-per-view receipts and the live gate. He had now, with Oscar's assistance, jumped into an income league occupied in the sport only by heavyweights and Mayweather. If general sports fans had been slow to place him before, they totally got the picture now. And though there were still capable opponents on the horizon for boxing's biggest little stars at that moment in December 2008, for the boxing public all around the globe, the evocative cosmic question was the one I faced over and over going forward. Because as the ringside blow-by-blow voice of what was at that time the sport's most prominent television stage, HBO, I had called almost all the meaningful fights that had served as the steps along the path to the inevitable and necessary confrontation.

So when were Floyd Mayweather and Manny Pacquiao going to fight each other?

The maddening answer was that it would take another six and a half years, until May 2, 2015, for their fight to finally occur. Why?

The answer ties together a variety of observations about what has happened to the modern world of sports, and how those interpretations affect athletes, their fans, the organizations that administer them, the teams and leagues, the massive financial forces that support them and feed off them, their media organizations that serve as middlemen to generate and count and distribute the money, the social media that are increasingly their proxy parties, and the hypesters and promoters of all kinds who focus their lenses on them.

Eventually, after years of parrying the unanswerable question, I called the largest single economic event in the history of what are now called "combat sports": Mayweather vs. Pacquiao—dubbed the Billion Dollar Bout for its unprecedented pay-per-view, advertising, merchandising, and ticket revenue.

You might have thought, based on years of nearly breathless anticipation, that would have been an unforgettably exciting moment. You would have been wrong. Seldom in my lengthy career was I more certain of the outcome of a competitive event I was narrating. Seldom have all the assembled media observers and experts surrounding me in that endeavor been more unified in their clear understanding of what they were about to see. Pacquiao was a shell of his former self and fought with an injured shoulder.

Remember, styles also make fights, and this was, as a style matchup, an open-and-shut case for Mayweather. But as the result of the extraordinary buildup, it was as "must see" as "must see" can get, and that is another observation, like all the ones listed above, on the inexorably interlocking dynamics of big-time sports in the 21st century.

Epilogue: Coming Home

"Debra Helped Me Say Goodbye to HBO" (Courtesy of Jim Lampley)

D ebra and I now live in Chapel Hill in a renovated farmhouse on six acres, which is large enough to entertain my growing family and special friends.

A couple of decades ago, a truly gifted American photographer named Howard Schatz developed (pun not intended) a deep interest in the world of boxing and the people who occupy it. The result was one of Howard's many distinctive photography books, a kaleidoscopic collection of boxing scenes and people titled *At the Fights*. I had the privilege of writing the foreword, and eventually as a gesture of brotherhood and gratitude, Howard offered to enlarge and mount for me any of the photos that deeply moved me. I chose two, and now in what feels like a triumph of counterintuition, they occupy the walls flanking the entry door to our peaceful Chapel Hill home.

One of them speaks to boxing's powerful psychic relationship with human suffering and redemption, and the reality that fighters spend much of their lives perched on the emotional razor's edge between victory and defeat. In 1984 Kassim Ouma was six years old in his tiny hometown in northern Uganda when a rebel militia truck rolled in and took all the first-grade boys away to fight. Like countless other child soldiers in the post-colonial Africa of that era, he endured and committed astonishing grisly atrocities over the next several years, first as a machete-slashing rebel insurgent, then, after being captured by the government army, a period of years chasing and murdering his former fellow rebels.

One day around age 20, Kassim saw a uniformed government soldier running outside the chain-link-fenced compound where he and his comrades were kept captive near the capital city of Kampala. He asked his commanding officer, "Hey, why does that guy get to run outside the fence?" The answer was, "Oh, he's on the boxing team. He's training." And instantly Kassim replied, "Hey, I'm a boxer, too."

Thus opened a new chapter in his challenged existence. Kassim began without skills, but given his deep immersion in suffering, opponents found it difficult to hurt or discourage him in the ring. Eventually on a team competition trip to the United States, he defected and wound up at a gym with aspiring professionals in West Palm Beach, Florida.

He went on a group excursion to a nightclub and was shot in the leg in a drive-by attack. Kassim Ouma had fought a war in Uganda for more than a dozen years but had to migrate to America to have the experience of being shot.

As a professional, he succeeded to a level far beyond where his skill set would have projected. Again, opponents found it hard to discourage him. He could go to war and subject himself to unwarranted punishment and sometimes wear down more gifted opponents. It was great television, and his premium pay-cable identity began.

Against all odds and devoid of world-class skills, Kassim Ouma won a recognized world title and fought for another one. By that often-misleading standard, his ring career can be seen as a success.

Thirteen years ago, in his 37th fight of a high-contact career, Kassim fought Kazakhstan's Gennady Golovkin, the most thunderously hard-punching middleweight of the past three decades. Golovkin was in the early stages of a 23-fight knockout streak, but Ouma made it to round 10 before the fight was stopped and Golovkin awarded a TKO. The struggle was a microcosm of his life. Since that time, mostly fighting in Europe, he has won twice and lost 10.

But he is alive, which in its way makes him more fortunate than the bulk of his cohorts and enemies in Uganda's endless civil war.

Not long after his loss to Golovkin, I spotted Kassim in Los Angeles, across the street from the Staples Center. Standing with Debra on the sidewalk a year and a half before we were married, I called out to Kassim, who instantly risked traffic havoc by racing to gleefully embrace me, whereupon I instantly introduced him to my newly beloved. Just as instantly, he pulled Debra into his arms for a sweet hello and spontaneously kissed her on the mouth. She was enthralled, and when he walked away she asked, of course, "Who was that?"

"Well, it's a great story. But the first thing I should tell you is that he's probably killed more people than either of us could count. And he killed them up close, with a machete."

"Oh my God. But he is so sweet!"

"Yes, he is. And life is truly strange, isn't it?"

He continues to live on our Chapel Hill wall.

The second photo in the hallway is there for familial reasons. Sergio Martínez was another junior middleweight I covered, a strikingly handsome and graceful Argentine southpaw who has lived much of his adult life in Spain. There were moments in his career when he was the best 154-pound fighter in the world, and I always loved covering him because of his facial resemblance to my older half-brother, Fred Trickey.

Fred was the first of my mother's two fatherless sons. Before he died of cancer, my father adopted Fred, who succumbed to AIDS around the time of our coincidental LA encounter with Kassim Ouma. But the familial connection to Sergio Martínez was due to his facial resemblance to Fred.

Martínez vs. Alex Bunema in Temecula, California, in 2008 was the second prizefight Debra attended with me. I wanted her to see that boxing could portray artistry and beauty, and Sergio, with gliding speed and magical hand skills, was the right example for that. I also wanted her to see his courage, another trait he shared with my brother, but for varied reasons.

Fred had come out as gay in the early 1960s in Hendersonville, North Carolina, when he was in his middle teens and remains the bravest person I ever knew. I could not look at Sergio Martínez, who was elegant and beautiful every moment amid the danger of prizefighting, without thinking of my brother. And at that moment as I watched Sergio, Fred was alive.

In 2015, Debra and I went to Canastota, New York, for my induction into the International Boxing Hall of Fame. It had indeed been something of a wait, given that I had now been calling fights at the highest levels of the sport for almost 30 years, but the wait was well worth it.

Aware that my career had often overshadowed my family, I was now overjoyed at the plan Debra had put together. For the first time since Grandma Mid's 100th birthday 25 years ago, all six surviving Lampley cousins from Hendersonville, along with my 90-plus-year-old aunt Mary Ann and uncle Bill, were in the same place at the same time.

The Hall of Fame had its annual vintage car parade around the town that produced lightweight and middleweight champion Carmen Basilio, and the inductees rode around in old convertibles, all of us waving and showing gratitude to Canastota for its love of boxing.

I shared induction that day with a proud assortment of deserving names, among them former welterweight champion and later actor Ray "Boom Boom" Mancini; journalist Nigel Collins, who had helped break me in, back in the '80s; Prince Naseem Hamed, who had introduced Victoria to boxing from the front row; and Riddick "Big Daddy" Bowe, whose heavyweight championship trilogy with Evander Holyfield was one of the greatest in the history of the sport, and a memorable part of my blow-by-blow legacy.

I kept calling fights, but in 2018 a seismic earthquake took place at HBO when the giant phone company AT&T decided a useful purpose for their cash might be to buy Time Warner, the historic entertainment conglomerate that decades before had developed and still owned HBO. That year I was at a post-Emmy party in Los Angeles, seated as had been the custom for a few years at the table of Richard Plepler, our beloved chairman. He tapped me on the shoulder and pointed to a business-suited figure a couple of tables away.

"See that man, the one in the gray suit and tie?"

"Yes, who is he?"

"That's John Stankey, your soon-to-be new boss. Once they take over [meaning AT&T], the sports department reports to him. You should go over and introduce yourself, see what you think."

To be clear, if Richard at that point in my life had told me to get a bucket of cow dung and pour it on the dance floor, I would have been out looking for a bucket of cow dung. Over four decades in television, I had never loved or respected an authority figure more. So I got up and walked over to the AT&T brass table and said hello, and Stankey invited me to sit down.

No more than 15 minutes later I walked back to the seat next to Plepler. "So how did that go?"

"I think boxing is over with. I don't think this network is going to be involved in it anymore."

"That is my impression, too. I just wanted to be sure we agree."

On December 8, 2018, in Carson, California, I called my last fight card for HBO Boxing.

The feature fight was a showcase for Cecilia Braekhus, the Norwegian fighter who was universally regarded as the best female boxer in the world. When it was over, Roy Jones, Max Kellerman, and I all made our personal goodbye comments from ringside, and with that, closing credits rolled and the most acclaimed telecast franchise in the 70-year history of boxing on television said goodbye.

I walked away from the eye of a network television camera for what could be the last time, forty-four years, three months, and a day after the first time.

In my more than 50 years as a network television sports broadcaster,

I watched at close range the evolution of all this and how it affected the games people play all around the world. I covered college football, pro football, professional golf, Major League Baseball, 14 Olympic Games— seven summer and seven winter—a dozen Wimbledon tennis championships, the esoterica of *Wide World of Sports'* "around the world, the constant variety of sport," the growth to maturity of extreme endurance sports, and some I can barely bring back to mind. The highs, memories, and thrills far outweigh the lows.

Like my life as a sportscaster, it was complicated. But "It Happened."

Acknowledgments

It Happened could not have told my story without 50-year friend Art Chansky; literary agent Adam Chromy; publisher Matt Holt; Katie, Lydia, Brigid, Jessika, Ariel, Kerri, Alicia, and Morgan of BenBella Books; Stefan Prelog, trusted adviser; publicist Fred Sternberg; the guidance of great friend and beloved author Thomas Hauser; the edits of Owen Davis; and the proofreading of Emily Kass.

And, above all, my loving and supportive wife, Debra, and our blended family.

Thanks to all for making *It Happened!*

—Jim Lampley

About the Authors

Photo by Anna Routh Barzin

Jim Lampley went from a small-town radio announcer to one of the most recognizable figures in the country as the first sideline reporter for nationally televised college football on ABC. From there his career expanded exponentially through *ABC's Wide World of Sports* and the start of 14 assignments at the Olympic Games and, fatefully, as the ABC boxing host, where he began to build his longest and most popular platform. After leaving ABC, he went to CBS and joined acclaimed co-anchor Bree Walker as among the first man and woman hosts of the evening news at KCBS in Los Angeles. His four-decade Olympics resume is the best in the business with assignments that included the "Miracle on Ice" in Lake Placid, the "Dream Team" in Barcelona, the bombing at Centennial Park in Atlanta, and turning the "Silent *Boléro*" at Sarajevo into among the most mesmerizing ice-skating events of all time. His 30-plus years with HBO included hosting Wimbledon weekday matches and becoming the face and voice of HBO Championship Boxing for 30 years that followed the rise and fall of Mike Tyson. He is still near ringside for ppv.com, hosting online chat sessions during the biggest bouts left in the sport. Lampley won three Emmys for boxing programming and was inducted into the International Boxing Hall of Fame in 2015. Jim lives in Chapel Hill, North Carolina, with his wife, Debra.

Art Chansky has been a sports reporter, broadcaster, columnist, and author for 50 years in North Carolina, where he and Lampley graduated from UNC-Chapel Hill. He has written 10 books, including bestsellers *The Dean's List*, *Blue Blood*, and *Game Changers*. He continues to broadcast, write, and sell for WCHL AM/FM radio, where he and Lampley met.